DARIO ROBLETO

SURVIVAL DOES NOT LIE IN THE HEAVENS

DES MOINES ART CENTER

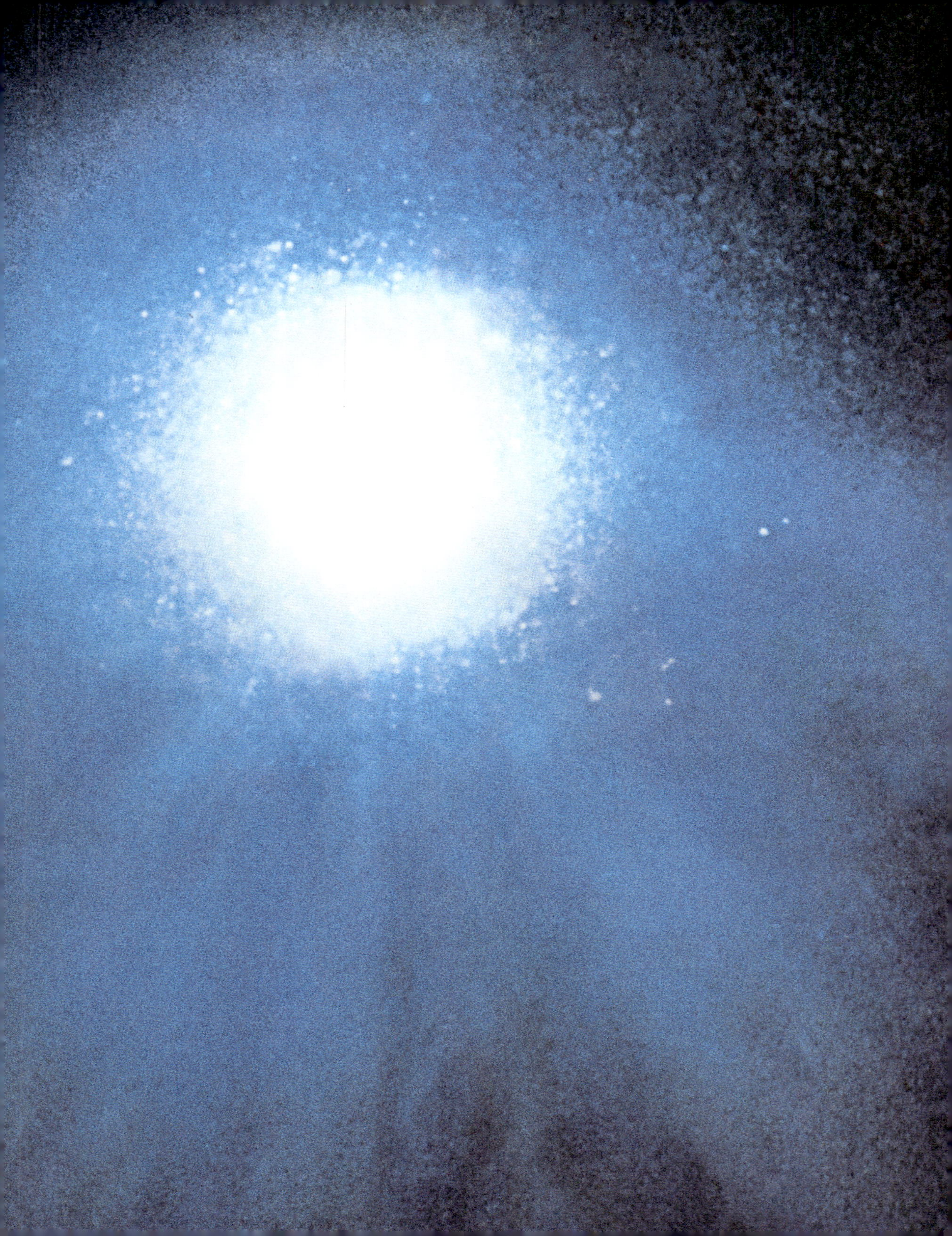

GILBERT VICARIO

WITH CONTRIBUTIONS BY

NAOMI ORESKES

MICHELLE WHITE

DES MOINES ART CENTER

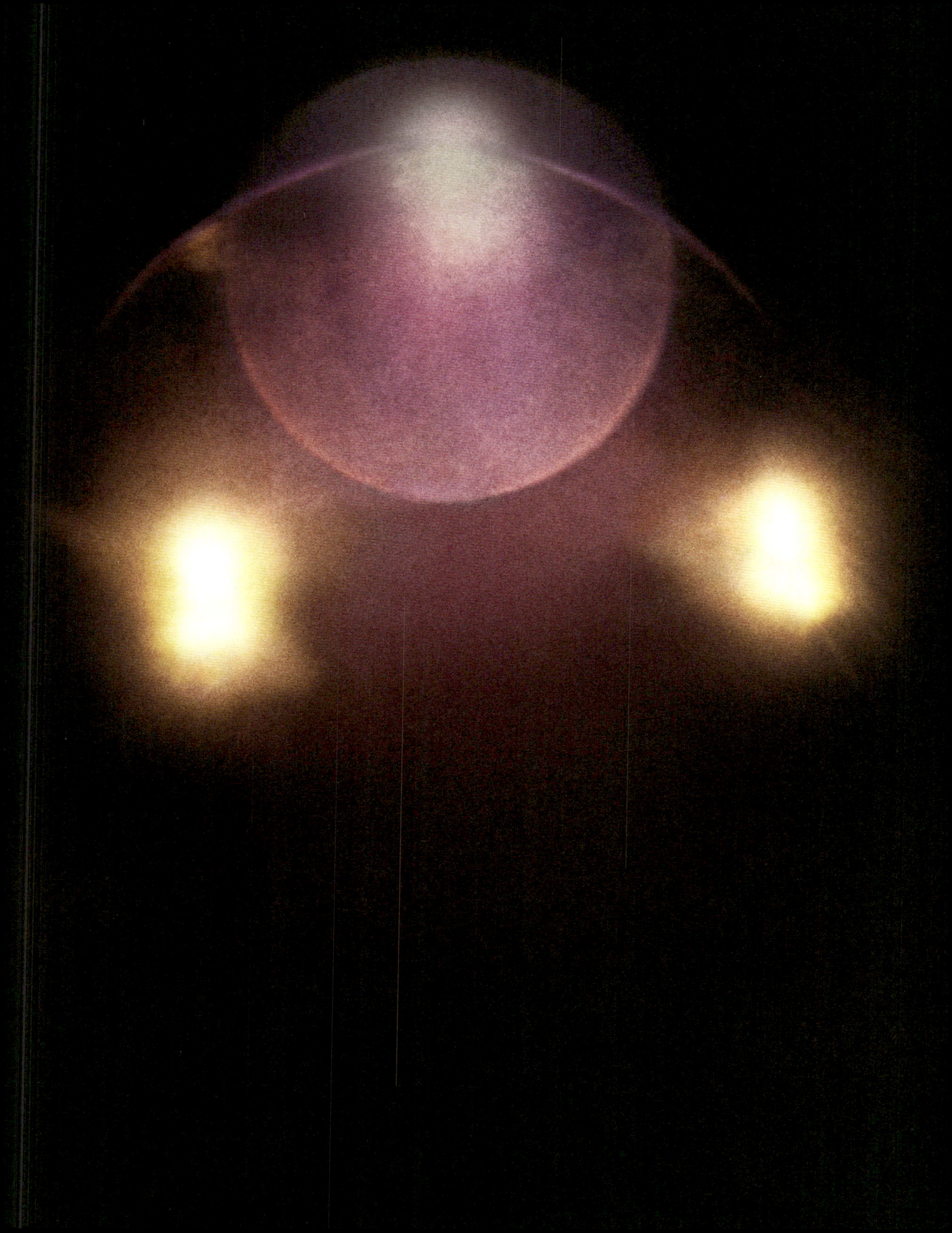

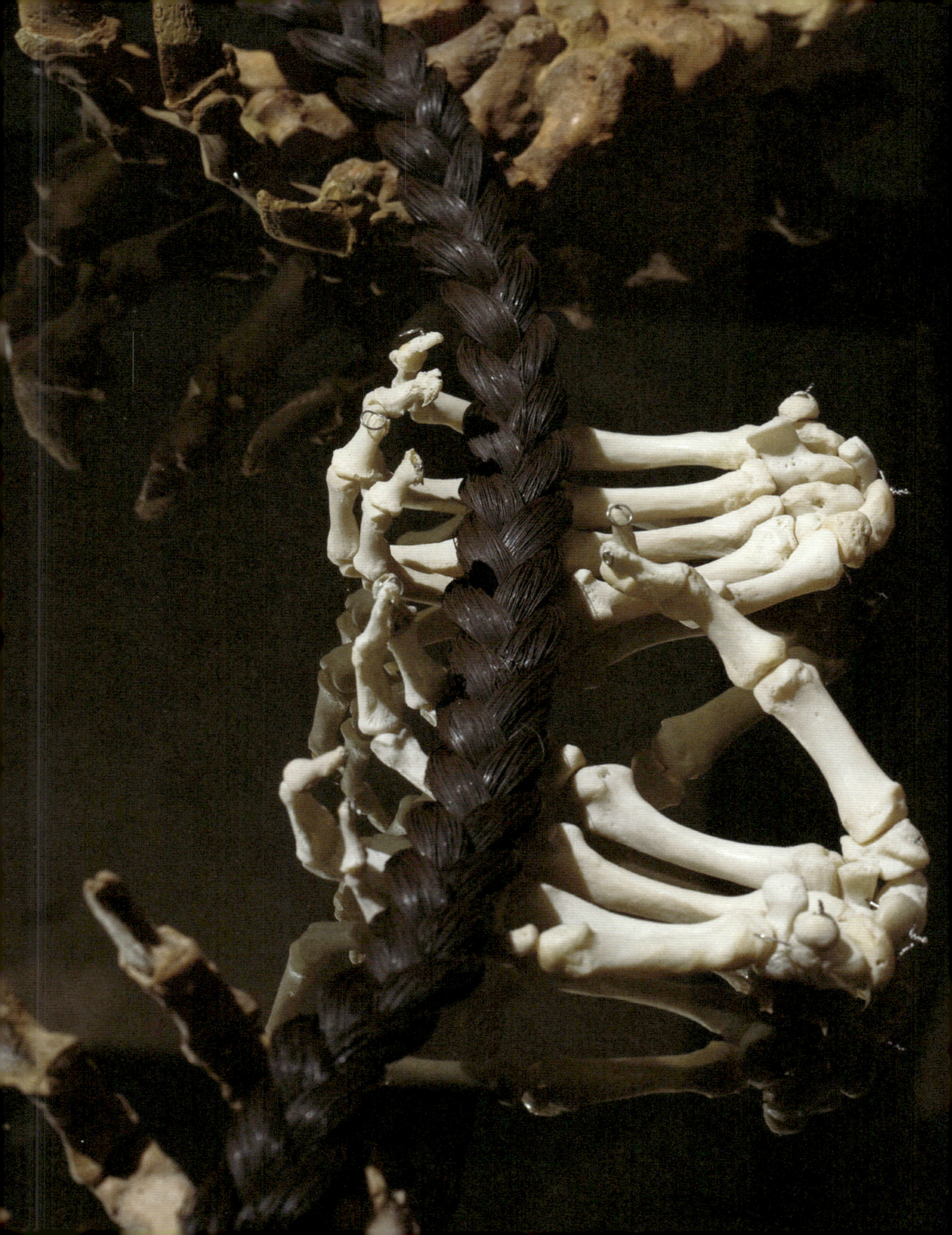

Jeff Fleming

DIRECTOR

Recently, a friend took part in an archeological dig in San Gemini, Italy. The activities there involved the excavation of the ancient Roman baths of Carsulae, a city that grew up around the Via Flaminia. She was allowed to bring home a small piece of clay roof tile from the hypocaust, the structural system produced by the Romans to circulate heat for the sauna. This rather odd-looking form of red clay appears to be unremarkable at first glance, but upon close inspection its function becomes clear, as does its connection to the past. One noteworthy aspect of this piece of clay is the obvious mark of a human finger as it moved across the wet surface before the tile was fired in a kiln. A human hand had touched and manipulated this clump of dirt 2,000 years ago. The form then functioned for perhaps several hundred years as part of a public structure, where it witnessed the comings and goings of thousands of individuals through peace and war, in plenitude and

THE COMMON DENOMINATOR OF EXISTENCE IS LOSS (DETAIL) 2008

famine. This clay bears a history. It carries memories for those who bother to investigate and becomes significant because of its connection to human life.

Dario Robleto examines this relationship between objects and experiences in his art. He looks for and investigates individual lives through the many items, functions, sounds, and smells that fill our communal existence. The Des Moines Art Center is especially proud of this project considering Robleto's idiosyncratic, obsessive, and laborious art. His work both infuses and extracts meaning from the objects that surround us; it is about the emotions that illustrate our humanity.

This exhibition continues the Art Center's ongoing commitment to younger artists who are making significant contributions to the dialogs surrounding the art of our time. I would like to thank the many individuals who made this project and its accompanying publication and programs possible. On the Art Center staff, Senior Curator Gilbert Vicario orchestrated the show beautifully; Associate Registrar Mickey Koch managed well the logistics of transportation; Chief Preparator Jay Ewart and his crew deftly installed and handled the artwork; and Director of Development Emily Bahnsen, Museum Education Director Jill Featherstone, and Marketing and Public Relations Director Christine Doolittle each handled their respective arenas with skill.

The funders for this project are the National Endowment for the

Arts and Wells Fargo. The Art Center is especially grateful for their support.

Lastly, I would like to thank Robleto for his enthusiasm for engaging wide audiences in our diverse community and for his willingness to share his examinations of the objects we harbor.

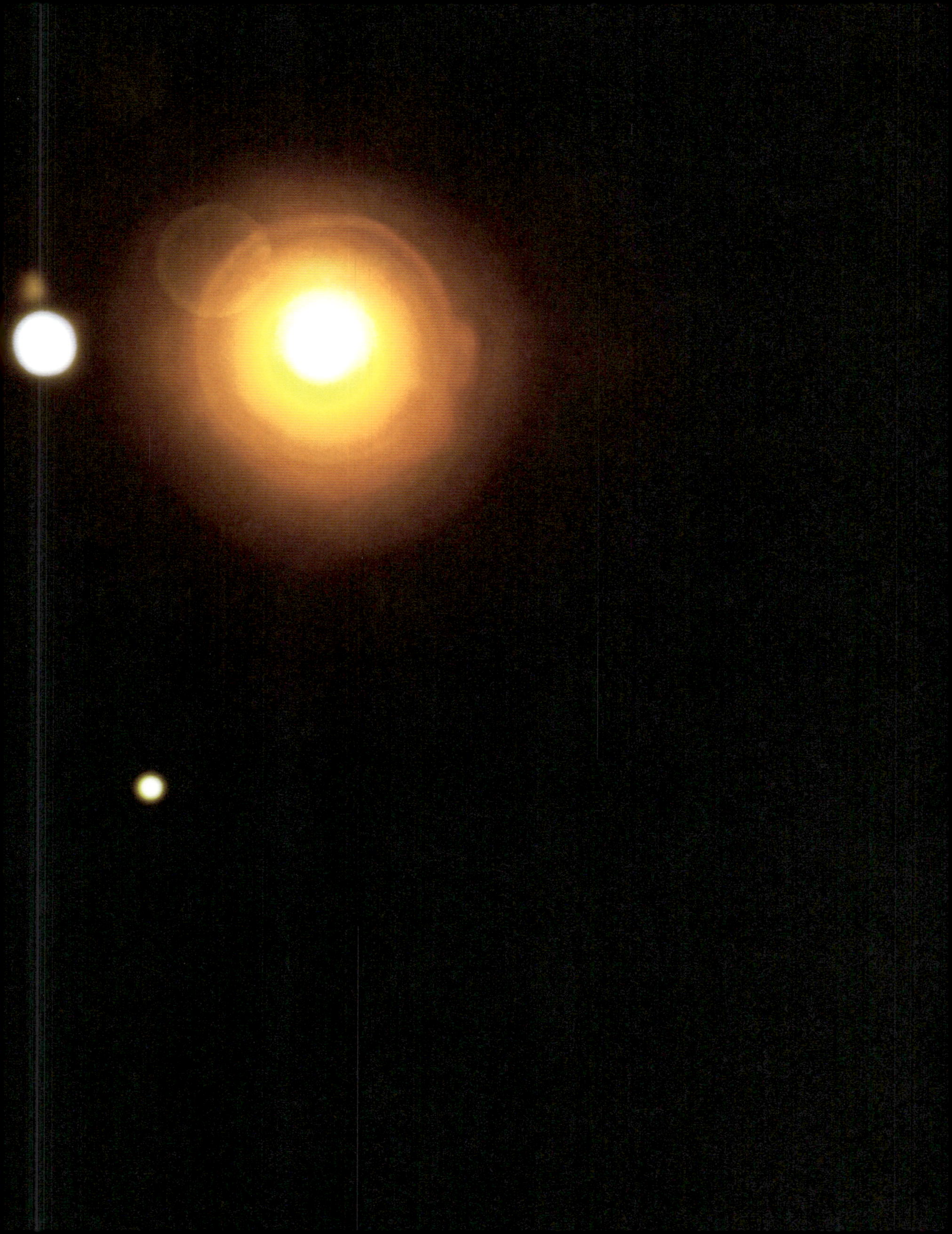

WE ARE MADE OF STARS

Gilbert Vicario

SENIOR CURATOR

Survival Does Not Lie In The Heavens examines Dario Robleto's current exploration of mortality and extinction through his incorporation of 19th-century folk traditions used to create visually arresting and densely layered objects. Faith and sentimentality are important components in Robleto's work and are exemplified through his use of evocative materials. These include vinyl records, dinosaur fossils, impact glass formed by meteorites, human tears, and heartbeats, to name a few. His use of language and text, however, remains an important component in its role as a descriptive, conceptual, and poetic bond between the objects and the meanings they elicit. A popular entry point into his use of language and text is perhaps best demonstrated through his abiding interest in popular music, which has informed his artistic process for well over a decade. The language and syntax of the music and the record industry—album cover artwork, song titles, B-sides, liner notes, remixes, mash-ups—are all used to create complex reverberations between the audible nature of music and objects that oftentimes contain elements that are invisible. Furthermore, his interest in how recording artists choose to identify themselves has led to a creative mash-up between his interest in science, human nature, and popular music. In fact, the title of the exhibition—*Survival Does Not Lie In The Heavens*—is taken from a work of art made in 2008, conceived of as an imagined tribute to citizen-scientists in the form of a collection of 45s. The song "Survival Does Not Lie In The Heavens" is by a group Robleto calls the Amateur Telescope Makers of Boston, a fictitious band he created along with the Chemistry Set and the Appalachian Botanical Club to form a collection of singles that pay tribute to amateur scientists. [FIG 1]

Such conceptual leaps are typical of Robleto, signifying a creative imagination that seems unusual in a moment when most contemporary art is driven by fact and not fiction. His wide-ranging interests, which include science, interpersonal relationships, spirituality, and history, have imbued his practice with an overarching humanistic tenor that seeks to question the ways in which meaning attaches itself to human-made objects. His use of language and text is a critical component to understanding these basic questions by complicating the relationship between the meaning of an object and the materials that go into the making of that object. This is a fundamental undercurrent of Robleto's artistic project and one that is clearly informed by specific precedents in contemporary art history. In particular, his

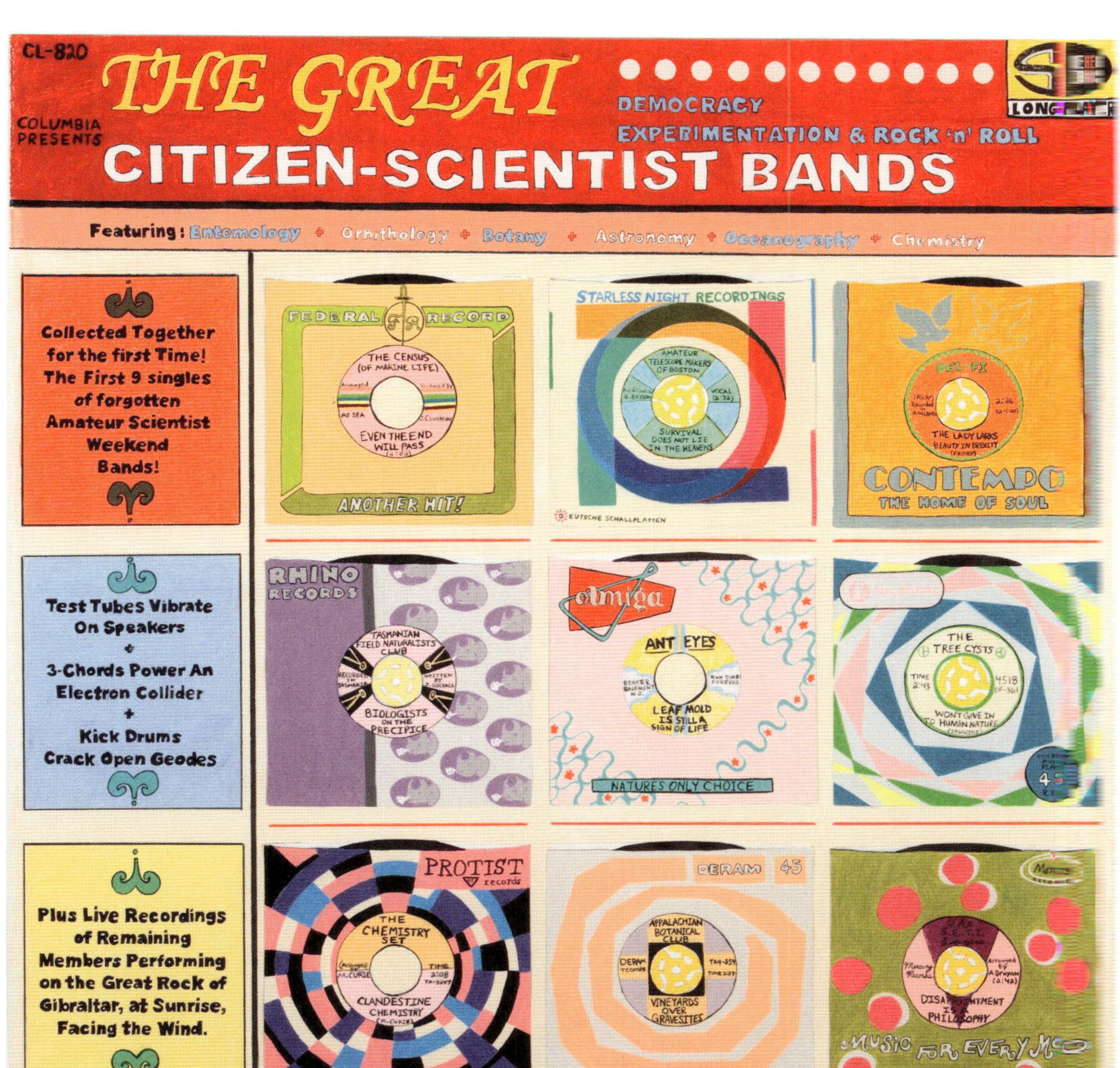

FIG 1 **THE CITIZEN-SCIENTIST BANDS** 2010

Colored pencil and marker on paper
30 x 30 inches
Collection of Marjorie and Michael Levine, New York

Be Mad, Be Rash, Smoke and Explode, Resist Or Move On

Sound waves, commotion

The Sex Pistols' Never Mind The Bollocks CD was,
through the aid of a computer program,
raised to a frequency level that is undetectable to human ears
and can only be heard by the animal world.
I then rode through my neighborhood for several nights
playing this tape at full volume with the windows down
creating a field of revolution to which only the animal world could respond.

Dimensions variable

1997

The Saddest Sounds I Can Imagine

Imagination, sounds in my head

Helen Keller singing Happy Birthday to herself, Patsy's voice as her plane descends,
Bob Dylan singing from the belly of a whale, the last Eunuch choir in the Vatican,
the heartbeat recording currently aboard Voyager I

Dimensions variable

1996

Billie Sings The Blues And Everything Matters

Compasses, magnets, altered magnetic field

Compasses purchased from a variety of places
(thrift stores, flea markets, garage sales, etc.)
were disassembled and, under the south poles of each compass
a tiny magnet was installed, keeping the dial perpetually pointing down.
The compasses were then returned to the spots from where they were purchased.

Dimensions variable

1997

understanding of conceptual art and the work of Felix Gonzalez-Torres, whose own work had a radical relationship between the intention of a work of art (in the conceptual sense) and its effect (how the work is physically manifest).

Robleto's practice clearly assimilates these lessons and their application toward a new relationship between the subject of a work and its physical appearance. One of his earliest series of works, *Oh, Those Mirrors with Memory* (Actions 1996–1997), [FIG 2] consists simply of the object labels themselves describing a particular action. This goes profoundly into the heart of conceptualism's roots by recalling the artistic strategy of Yoko Ono, whose famously Zen-like pieces such as *Hide and Seek* (1964) prompted viewers with instructions that were ultimately intended to be completed in the minds of the viewer and potentially outside the confines of the exhibition space. "Hide until everybody goes home. Hide until everybody forgets about you. Hide until everybody dies." In Robleto's version, it is his actions that are documented, leaving it up to the viewer to reconstruct in his or her imagination how these could potentially play out.

The element of doubt or uncertainty that the viewer might experience with this body of work has only increased in subsequent works. In fact, one might say that this destabilizing factor has become part of Robleto's conceptual ammunition to further underscore the nature of meaning and

FIG 2 Exerpts from OH, THOSE MIRRORS WITH MEMORY (ACTIONS 1996–1997)

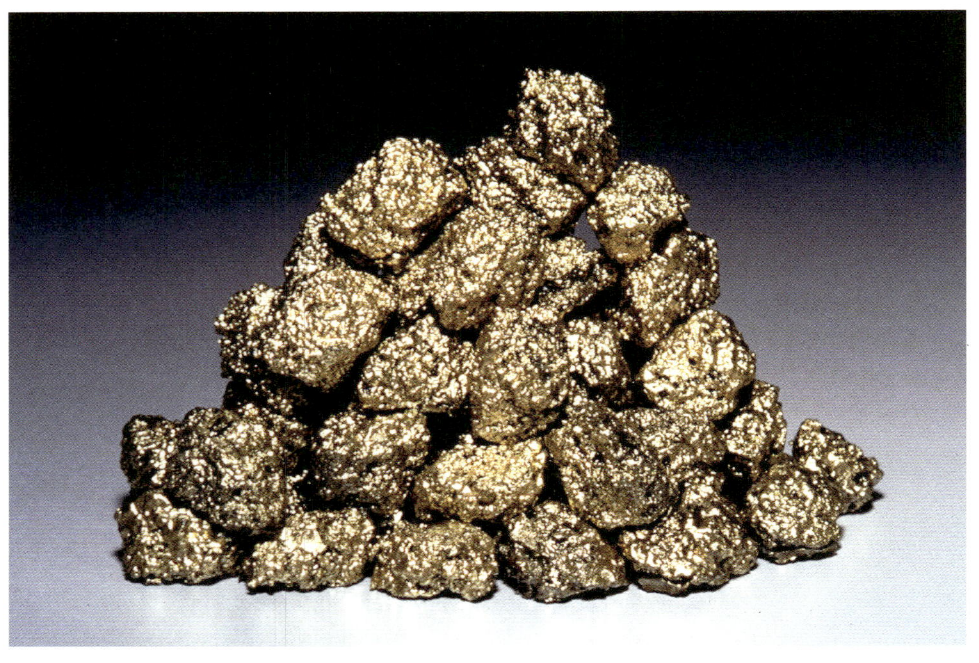

how that becomes signified within a particular work of art. His practice of embedding music and lyrics into an object, for example, demonstrates his unique alchemical process of taking audiotape or vinyl records and converting them into physical objects. As an example, *Jimmie, Your Cheeks Will Never Lose Their Luster* (1998) is made of dissolved magnetic audiotape, resin, hand-set amethyst crystals, and paint along with the following explanatory text: Geode rock created from a dissolved magnetic audiotape recording of Jimi Hendrix's guitar distortion sampled from his track "Purple Haze." Another work, titled *I Saw a Pop Idol Sneer at a Dying Kid* (1998), [FIG 3] is made of melted vinyl record, resin, and spray paint and includes the following explanatory text: A used, thrift-store copy of Michael Jackson's album *Thriller* was melted down and shaped into nuggets of iron pyrite (fool's gold) makes the most literal connection to the ancient tradition of alchemy and its associations with myth, religion, and spirituality.

In 1999, he created three sculptures cast out of thrift-store trophy parts and melted vinyl records: *I Wish I Could Give Aretha All the R.E.S.P.E.C.T. She Will Ever Need* (made with melted 45s of Aretha Franklin's "You Make Me Feel Like a Natural Woman," "Prove It," and "Chain of Fools"), *I Wish I Could Give Kraftwerk All the Soul They Will Ever Need* (made with melted vinyl records of Kraftwerk's "Computer World," "The Man Machine," and "Trans Europe Express"), and *I Wish I Could Give Maria All the Soul She Will Ever Need* (made with vinyl records of live recordings of Maria Callas singing in *Norma*, *Madame Butterfly*, and *Tosca*) that reverberate between the collective memory of those recordings and their entombment within the slightly pathetic body of the high school trophy. [FIG 4]

In the last decade, history has begun to play a bigger role in the evolution of Robleto's work, bringing a more profound way of exploring

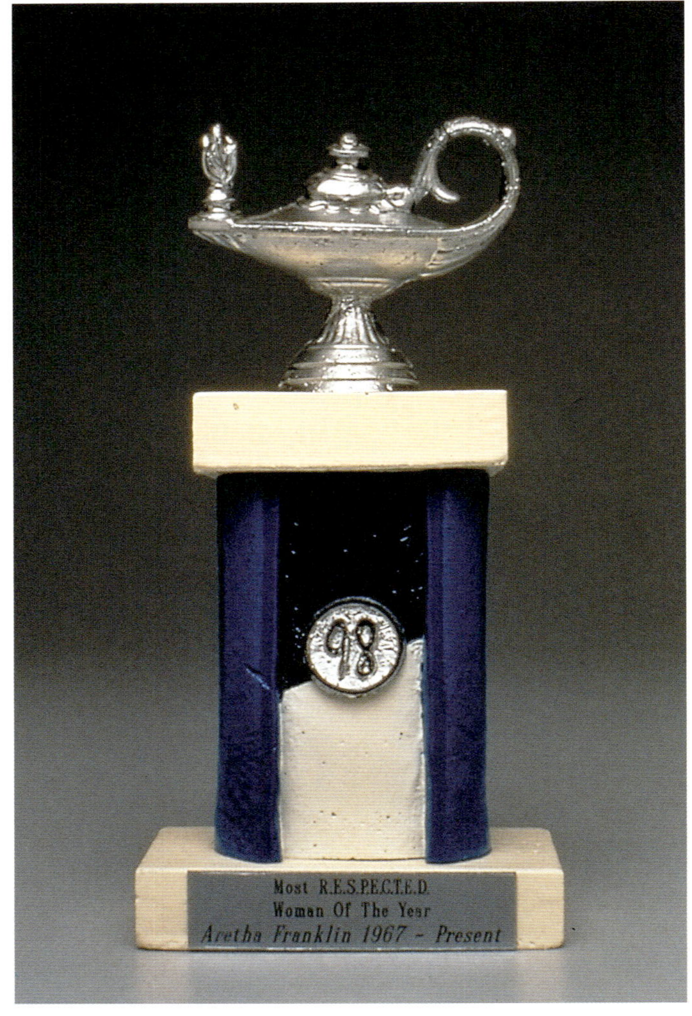

FIG 4 **I WISH I COULD GIVE ARETHA ALL THE R.E.S.P.E.C.T. SHE WILL EVER NEED** 1999

Cast of found and thrift-store trophy parts made with melted
Aretha Franklin 45 rpm records ("You Make Me Feel Like A Natural Woman,"
"Prove it," "Chain of Fools"), resin, spray paint, engraved silver label
8 x 3 x 2 inches
Collection of The Museum of Fine Arts, Houston, selected by Jereann and Holland Chaney,
gift of Leslie and Brad Bucher in memory of Robert Chaney

human connections and emotional bonds. A significant portion of work during this period begins to develop around his interest in various wars and how that relates to his ongoing exploration of emotional and physical attachments. In a 2008 interview with Ian Berry, Robleto explains, "The First World War brought with it an unprecedented level of destruction. For the first time in history, you could literally destroy a whole person on the battlefield, leaving nothing behind. This threw mourning customs into havoc, especially for people in some of the Catholic countries who had so much invested in mourning a body, or properly burying something. It led to a moment in which a whole generation of families did not know how to mourn properly and were torn apart by it. I'm drawn to these beautiful moments when people rise up to fill a hole that has been created by tragedy."[i]

Robleto's approach to creating objects that carry such a heavy burden of signification can be as startling and visceral as the heavyweight subject matter can bear. His overarching interest in exploring how objects are imbued with meaning takes on a whole new level of commitment, resolutely challenging the boundaries between art as a purely Aristotelian endeavor and coaxing it into the social imaginary through the development of an ongoing fictional narrative. The emotional tension of his statement is met head-on by the visceral materials used in works such as *No One Has A Monopoly Over Sorrow* (2004–2005), [FIG 5] which includes men's wedding ring finger

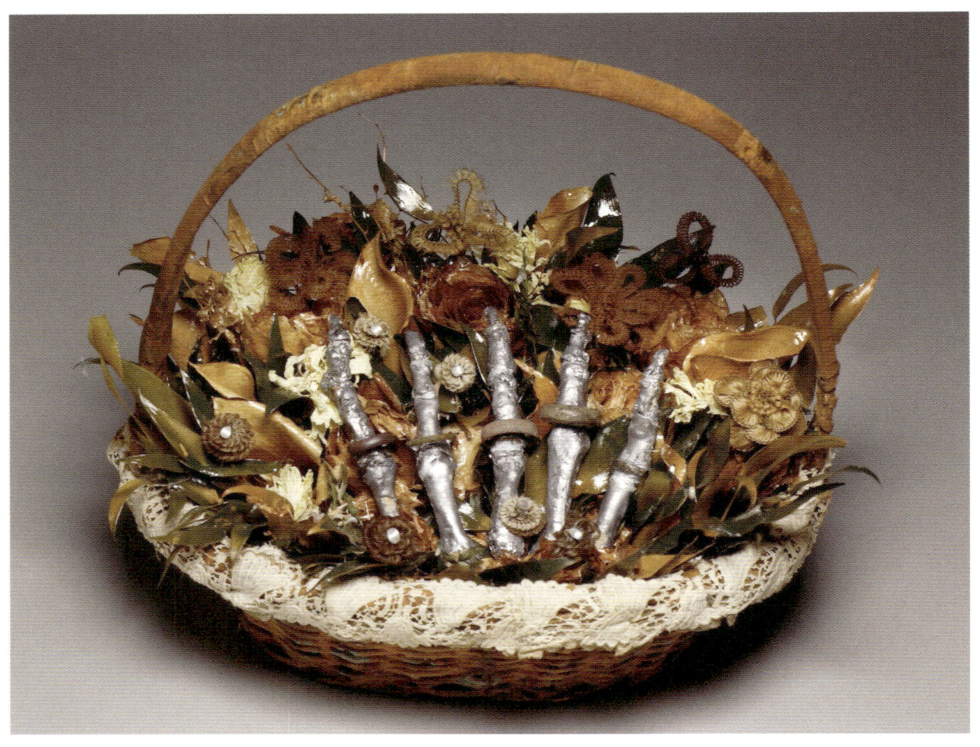

Men's wedding ring finger bones coated in melted bullet lead from
various American wars, men's wedding bands excavated from American battlefields,
melted shrapnel, wax dipped preserved bridal bouquets of roses and white calla lilies
from various eras, dried chrysanthemums, male hair flowers braided by a
civil war widow, fragments from a mourning dress, cold cast brass, bronze, zinc,
and silver, rust, mahogany, glass
11 x 10 x 9 inches
Collection of Julie Blakeslee, Austin, Texas

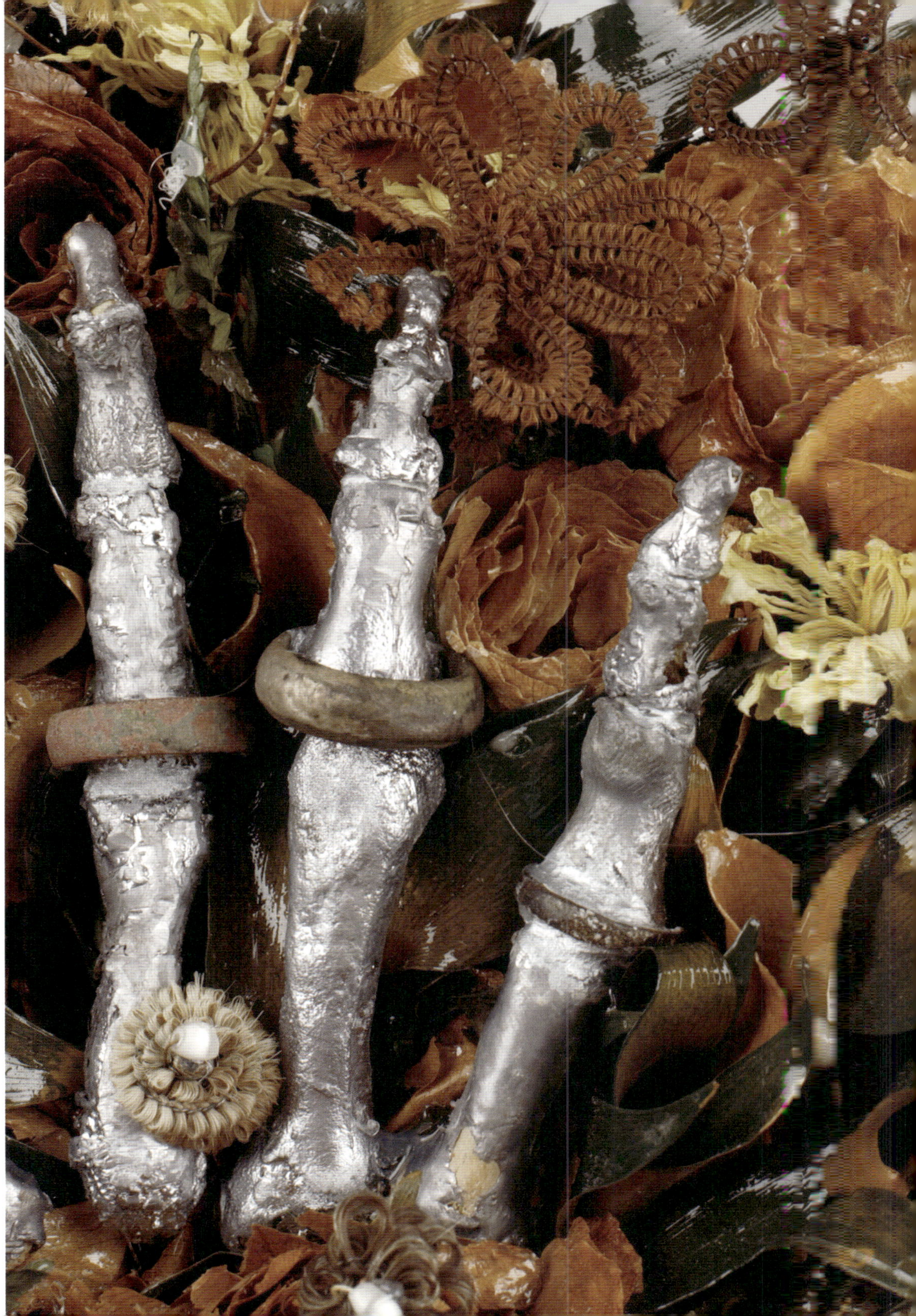

bones coated in melted bullet lead from various American wars, men's wedding bands excavated from American battlefields and melted shrapnel. Another ubiquitous component found in his war works is homemade paper containing pulp made from soldiers' letters, such as in the wreath collage titled *Greenville Sanitary Fair* (2005), [FIG 6] which was made in tribute to the Civil War volunteer efforts of American women who worked as nurses, ran kitchens in Army camps, and raised money for funds and supplies. Here, his transformation of the letters into material used to construct his paper collages is closely aligned with his abiding interest in the transmutability of materials—effectively transforming their original appearance in an effort to preserve and underscore their symbolic potency.

Robleto's recent projects, and specifically those that comprise the exhibition *Survival Does Not Lie In The Heavens*, continue to address the tensions between content, materiality, and language. The principle of transmutation[1] as an existentialist condition, as seen in the earlier melted-vinyl pieces, seems to give way, however, to larger questions that dramatically highlight the evanescence of time and memory. Postmillennial issues such as global warming, climate change, and the end of the world come strikingly into play in his recent works. They become dramatically materialized by intentionally sidestepping rationalist, contemporary forms

---

1 Transmutation: to change into another nature substance, form, or condition.

and idioms, and instead they readily appropriate pre-20th-century artistic practices. Victorian steamer trunks, 19th-century hair jewelry, medical cupping equipment, and vials of homeopathic preparations are presented as conceptual objects dressed as historic artifacts. Many of these items are in fact handmade by the artist as way of resuscitating lost art forms and bringing them into a present-day discourse. The subjects contained within these pieces—the disappearance of animal species, glacial ice melts, sickness, and human supercentenarians—provide the basis for Robleto's current interest in both extinction and longevity by creating an almost paradoxical union between sentimentality and human emotions within the realm of scientific objectivity and reason.

Some Longings Survive Death (2008), for example, highlights the discovery of 50,000-year-old woolly mammoth tusks through the process of glacial melting. The shadow box is modeled after a 19th-century one and contains authentic Victorian hair work such as intricately braided hair flowers, lockets, and brooches, hair work made by the artist, and more than 100 strands of woolly mammoth hair. In Europe, and in particular France, Germany, and England, the traditional use of hair as an ornamental object was a popular art form beginning in the 17th century. Cherished as a privileged human relic, hair was braided, plaited, incorporated into portrait miniatures, and mounted into brooches and pendants to mark significant life events such

FIG 6 GREENVILLE SANITARY FAIR 2005

Homemade paper (pulp made from soldiers' letters
home from various wars, ink retrieved from letters, cotton), colored paper,
thread and fabric from soldiers' uniforms from various wars, carte de visites,
silk, ribbon, wood clothespins, pen, foam core, poplar, ash
38 x 32 x 3 1/2 inches
Collection of Lois and Louis Fingerman, Des Moines, Iowa

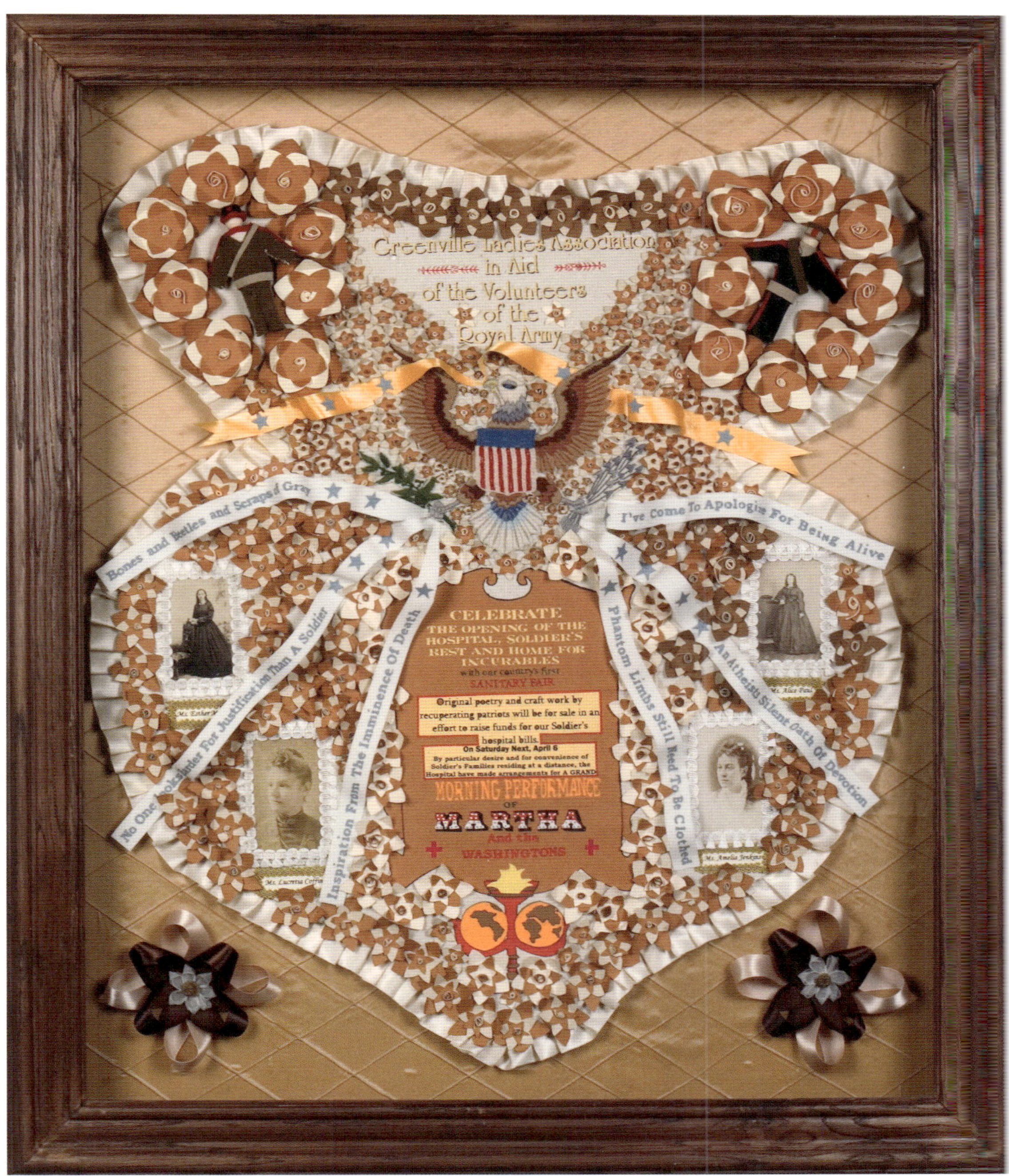

Greenville Ladies Association
in Aid
of the Volunteers
of the
Royal Army

Bones and Bottles and Scraps of Grey
I've Come To Apologise For Being Alive
No One Is Sadder For Justification Than A Soldier
Inspiration From The Imminence Of Death
Phantom Limbs Still Need To Be Clothed
An Atheist's Silent Oath Of Devotion

CELEBRATE
THE OPENING OF THE
HOSPITAL, SOLDIER'S
REST AND HOME FOR
INCURABLES
with our country's first
SANITARY FAIR

Original poetry and craft work by
recuperating patriots will be for sale in an
effort to raise funds for our Soldier's
hospital bills.
On Saturday Next, April 6
By particular desire and for convenience of
Soldier's Families residing at a distance, the
Hospital have made arrangements for A GRAND
MORNING PERFORMANCE
OF
MARTHA
And the
WASHINGTONS

Ms. Esther W.
Ms. Alice Paul
Ms. Lucretia Coffin
Ms. Amelia Jenkyns

as births, betrothals, and deaths. In particular, the use of hair in mourning jewelry had particular appeal. Cynthia Amnéus writes, "[A] lock of hair was a natural inclusion in mourning or memorial jewelry. Its use as a memento mori dates to the late 17th century. Hair was the one part of the loved one, save for less enchanting fingernail clippings or teeth, that could serve in memoriam as a sentimental keepsake." The arrangement of these objects in the shadow box collapses the enormous expanse of time from when woolly mammoths roamed the earth and relates it to our own customs and norms for commemorating deceased relatives.

Geological issues of time, materials, and life cycles serve as potent signposts for this new millennium that guide Robleto's thinking down the path of acknowledging and lamenting that which occurred in the past. It is through this threshold of an *a priori*[2] scientific knowledge base that past, present, and future become inextricably linked through a singular practice that is increasingly tethered to scientific tropes and fictional narratives used to express a reaction to a loss that can no longer be recovered. In *Words Tremble With the Thoughts They Express* (2008), Robleto compares human languages and animals that no longer exist. The feathers are made of stretched audiotape containing the voices of four lost human languages and the last

---

2 A priori: known to be true independently of or in advance of experience of the subject matter; requiring no
   evidence for its validation or support.

recordings of extinct birds. Through this piece, the artist addresses the fact that the forces that push a particular animal to extinction are the same forces at work in the demise of certain languages. The writing quills and homemade ink consisting of lamp black, ground fulgurites [glass produced by lightning strikes when heat from the blast melts surrounding sand], and cuttlefish sepia exemplify the missing link between the lost voices and our own. Similarly, in *The Common Denominator of Existence Is Loss* (2008), he addresses the first incidence of human-induced extinction, which scientists believe was a particular species of the cave bear during the Pleistocene era. Using actual fossil remnants of cave bear paws and human hands, Robleto creates a ring out of what appears to be a Victorian hair braid to speak about this particular moment. The hair braid is actually a stretched and pulled audiotape of an early recording of an experimental clock, which Robleto uses as a metaphor to suggest the possibility of cheating death through technology.

Two metaphorically conjoined pieces, *The Boundary of Life Is Quietly Crossed* (2008) and *The Ark of Frailty* (2008), perhaps most succinctly address the artist's interest in extinction and our own mortality. Designed to look like a Victorian-era vitrine, *The Boundary of Life Is Quietly Crossed* celebrates human supercentenarians — people who live to at least 110 years of age — through an arrangement of plaques dedicated to individuals who have surpassed that threshold. Details of the individuals are given, including name, age, and places of birth and death, along with biographical information detailing the person's life. The plaque titled "Time Wraps Around Your Tears" celebrates the life and death of Eva Morris, a resident of Staffordshire, England, who died six days short of her 115th birthday. The plaque goes on to state that her "life spanned three centuries and attributed her longevity to whiskey and boiled onions." The bottom of the plaque has her birth and death dates, November 8, 1885 – November 2, 2000, as well as the dates she held the record for being the world's oldest person, December 30, 1999 – November 2, 2000. Every time a new record holder is identified, Robleto creates a commemorative plaque and adds it to the bottom right corner of the case. In the second piece, *The Ark of Frailty*, a series of plaques similarly presented in a Victorian-era vitrine pays tribute to animal species thought to be extinct but were later rediscovered. Each plaque commemorates a Lazarus species,[3] one that has seemingly risen from the dead, with the earliest discovery occupying the upper lefthand corner and the most recent discovery occupying the lower righthand corner. One plaque, for example, commemorates the rediscovery of *Galliota gomerona*, a giant lizard indigenous to the Canary Islands that was thought to have gone extinct around 1500 but was rediscovered in 1999. Taken together, these

---

3   A Lazarus species is commonly defined as an organism that is rediscovered alive after having been widely considered extinct for years. Not to be confused with an Elvis species (a lookalike species). Wikipedia.org.

pieces attempt to examine the Darwinian principle of survival of the fittest while foreshadowing the possibility of human extinction.

Concurrently, Robleto's interest in archaic medical notions and scientific equipment, such as homeopathic treatments and cupping instruments, looks back at a crucial moment in our early modern history when the rational perception of the body, both through medical and scientific practices, began to take shape. *A Homeopathic Treatment for Human Longing* (2008) references three systems of medical procedures including phlebotomy, or bloodletting; electric shock; and the practice of homeopathy used to treat physical illnesses. The large presentation case, which resembles an old-fashioned steamer trunk, holds vintage glass vials, glass electrode wands, and 19th-century bloodletting cupping glasses combined with custom-ordered homeopathic remedies. The ingredients in Robleto's formulations — sound of glaciers melting, voice of oldest to ever live, last heartbeats of loved one, million-year-old blossom, million-year-old raindrop, deceased lovers' heartbeats, black swan bone dust, Sylvia Plath's voice — almost resemble free-verse poetry and ultimately blur the line between empirical knowledge and that which we take on faith to be true. Here, as in other works, Robleto juxtaposes scientific instruments that were intended to correct the inner workings of the body with ephemeral and highly emotive contents to express a paradoxical disconnection between our physical bodies and the memories and experiences they contain.

A self-described materialist poet, Robleto's work, such as in *A Homeopathic Treatment for Human Longing*, convincingly expresses the ephemeral nature of human longing and emotional connections. Yet as his work progresses, he continues to pose the problem of how an object acquires meaning and symbolic potency. This preoccupation reinforces his connection to the fundamental principles of conceptual art by creating works whose meanings are mediated by text. These important sources of information provide the crucial link between how one receives the meaning behind a work of art and the object itself; but also call into question the ability of an object to stand on its own. One way this is done is by using the structure of an object label, as seen in his work since the mid-1990s, to deliver a crucial component of a work's overall meaning. Aside from providing this raw data of information on the materials used, the sheer range of components—from conventional artist's materials to organic substances to exotic ephemera—elicits a rhythmic and evocative subtext to the object in reference. In the current work, it clearly enables one to "see" things that cannot be read by the human eye; the object label therefore functions as a textual microscope, enabling one a super-vision onto a particular work of art.

This layering of information and meaning creates a poetic density that builds its own narrative—far from the mere facts and materials used to make a work of art. It is through this process that Robleto begins to create his own metaphorology[4], a term originally coined in 1960 by the German philosopher Hans Blumenberg as a way of understanding things that cannot be explained through mere reason or proof. In art historian Barbara Maria Stafford's book *Body Criticism: Imagining the Unseen in Enlightenment Art and Medicine*, she elaborates on the term:

> "Metaphorology, then, opens up a wider and truly cross-disciplinary horizon onto the past and the future. It permits us to rethink, reformulate, and perhaps even constructively reshape the abiding yet changing problem of the relationship of image to text, imagination to reason, and body to soul. It recognizes the existence of multiple intelligences, not just the specious communism of a single intellectual competence."[ii]

Robleto's work clearly finds a kindred spirit in this statement by allowing the seemingly incompatible realms of knowledge to coexist within a new narrative construction. His cross-disciplinary approach to sculpture, encompassing elements of conceptualism, material history, folk narratives,

---

4 Blumenberg created what has come to be called 'metaphorology', which states that what lies under metaphors and language modisms, is the nearest to the truth (and the farthest from ideologies). The term was the basis of his 1960 book *Paradigms for a Metaphorology*.

and popular music, allows him to play with the suppleness of language and materials in many unexpected ways. This dialectic also informs his works on paper to constitute a critical component of his overall artistic project. Serving as an agitprop and promotional backdrop to his interest in meaning and materials are his works on paper that articulate and further many of these concerns by providing multiple perspectives created through fictional communities and organizations. Works like *Alchemical Gardens, Folks on the Fringe, Society of Seekers,* and *Maidens of Mother's Milk Thistle* (2009) pay homage to the posters of the WPA (Works Progress Administration) of the 1930s that were originally designed to publicize health and safety programs; cultural programs including art exhibitions and theatrical and musical performances; travel and tourism; educational programs; and community activities. In Robleto's versions, each pays tribute to a specific aspect of our collective desires and aspirations, and spins a metaphoric and hopeful narrative on society, culture, and survival.

In two recent works, Robleto leaves behind the material traces of our past, used so effectively in his object-making, and returns to the lexicon of the album cover to create work that looks toward metaphysics and the potential consequences of eternal life. In *Tales of Theodicies* (2010), a monumental paper collage of imagined album covers, mortality and survival is addressed through an examination of the intrinsic nature of

God's existence and his inability to eradicate evil.[5] Each of Robleto's panels, which focus on individual prison choirs in actual prisons across the country, follows the design logic of the album cover, from graphic design, branding elements, and company logos to album titles and songs. The Louisiana State Penitentiary in Angola, for example, is represented by the Tongueless Poet of Cellblock 9 singing "Things Placed in the Sea, Become the Sea," while the Pentonville Men's Prison Choir sings such hits as "Evil is a Mystery We Don't Care to Solve" and "Is Evil Something I Am Or Something I Do?"— effectively contaminating the transcendent power of gospel music with themes that cast philosophical doubt on redemption and the afterlife. In *Candles Un-burn, Suns Un-shine, Death Un-dies* (2011), Robleto creates an immersive constellation of solar masses and heavenly bodies that plays on the mythic status of the dead artist. In reality, this site-specific wallpaper installation is composed of digital collages of stage lights taken from the album covers of live performances of now-deceased musicians. Stage lights that once bathed the faces and bodies of recording artists such as Johnny Cash, John Coltrane, Jimi Hendrix, Billie Holiday, Lightnin' Hopkins, and T. Rex remain an evanescent and spiritual connection to their physical selves. Through this digital process he creates a virtual pantheon of "voices" that

---

5 Theodicy is a specific branch of theology and philosophy that attempts to reconcile belief in God
   with the perceived existence of evil. Wikipedia.org.

continues to inspire Robleto's unique practice. In *Candles Un-burn*, his preoccupation with mortality, as seen in previous work, moves toward a new way of depicting eternal life through the lingering traces of light and space. The obtuse referencing of language and text through popular music engages our own experiences and emotions through the memories elicited by those songs while suggesting the possibility of our own transcendence. In Robleto's ceaseless exploration of our bodies and the memories they contain he continues to remind us of the fleeting nature of life. By engaging in a conceptual practice that connects the knowledge of the past with the uncertainty of the future through objects, language, and customs, we are obliged to acknowledge our fundamental nature. We are made of stars.

ENDNOTES

i   Berry, Ian. "Medicine On The Spoon: A Dialogue with Dario Robleto," in *Dario Robleto: Alloy of Love*.
    University of Washington Press and The Frances Young Tang Teaching Museum and Art Gallery, Skidmore
    College: New York, 2008. p. 258.

ii Stafford, Barbara Maria. *Body Criticism: Imagining the Unseen in Enlightenment Art and Medicine*.
    The MIT Press: Cambridge, Massachusetts, 1991. p. 7.

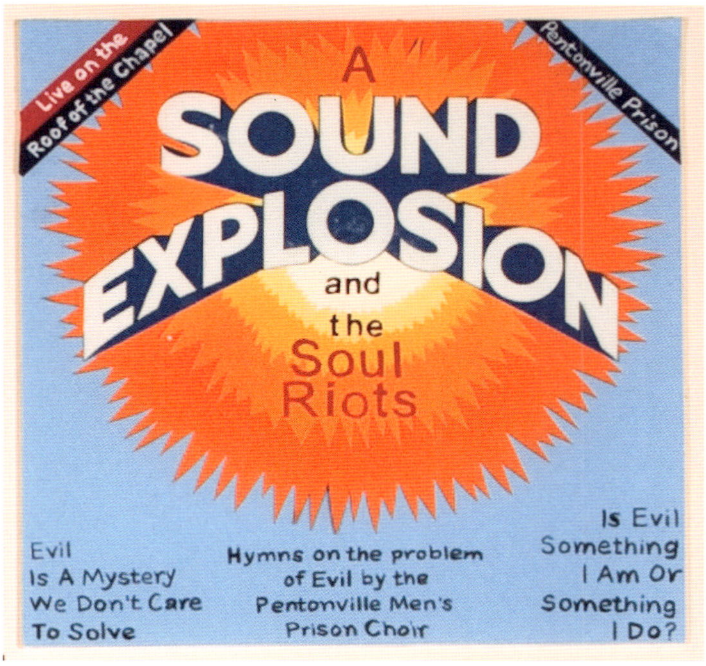

TALES OF THEODICIES 2010 (detail)

Cut paper, cut album cover elements, colored pencil,
ribbon, foam core, glue

DARIO ROBLETO

SURVIVAL DOES NOT LIE IN THE HEAVENS

DEFIANT GARDENS 2009-2010

Cut paper, homemade paper (pulp made from soldiers' letters
sent home and wife/sweetheart letters sent to soldiers from various
wars, cotton), carrier pigeon skeletons, WWII-era pigeon message
capsules, dried flowers from various battlefields, hair flowers
braided by war widows, mourning dress fabric, excavated shrapnel
and bullet lead from various battlefields, various seeds,
various seashells, cartes de visites, gold leaf, silk, ribbon,
wood, glass, foam core, glue

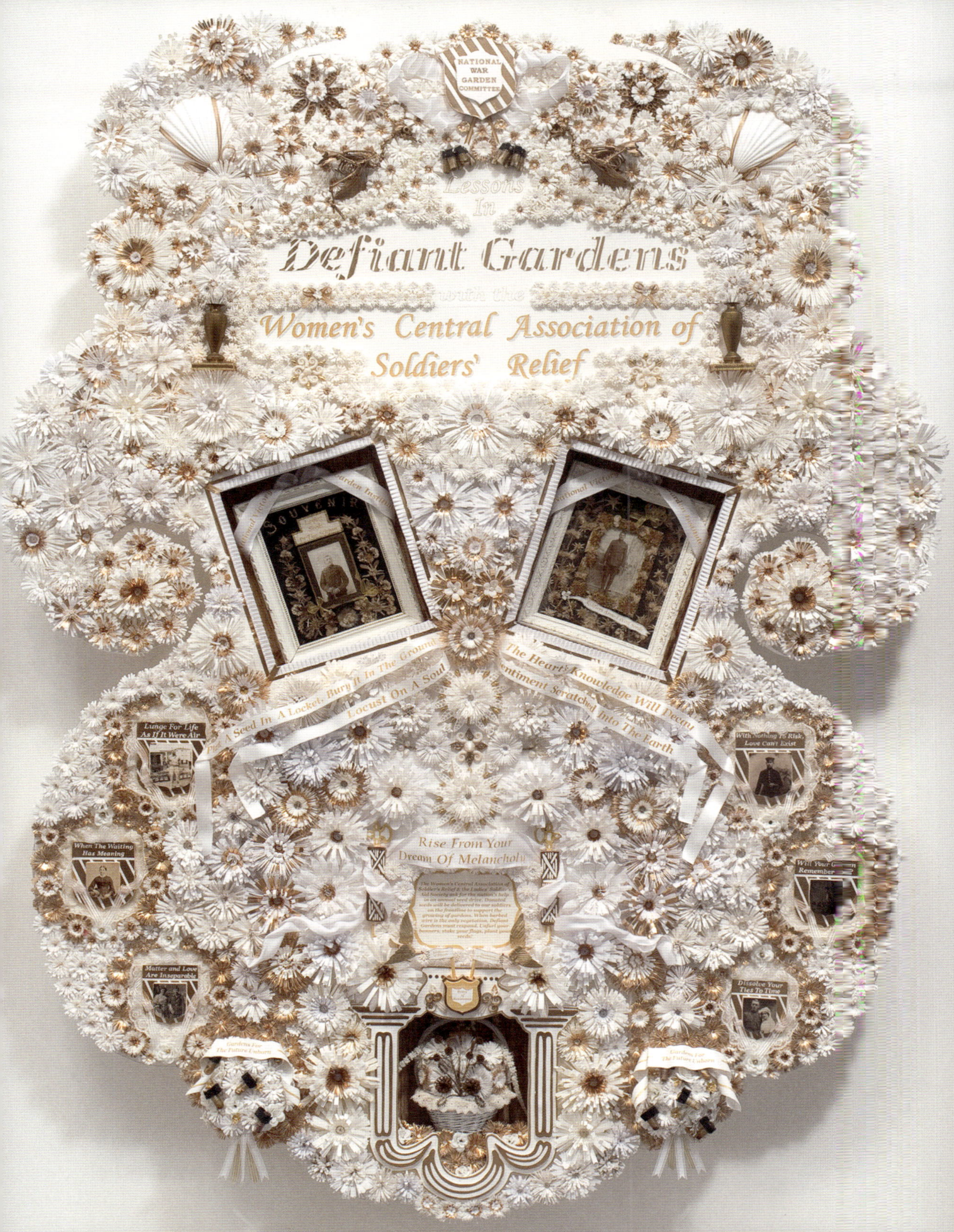

NATIONAL WAR GARDEN COMMITTEE
Lessons In
Defiant Gardens
with the
Women's Central Association of Soldiers' Relief
SOUVENIR
Plant A Seed In A Locket, Bury It In The Ground
Locust On A Soul
The Heart's Knowledge Will Decay
Sentiment Scratched Into The Earth
Lunge For Life As If It Were Air
With Nothing To Risk, Love Can't Exist
When The Waiting Has Meaning
Rise From Your Dream Of Melancholy
Will Your Garden Remember
Matter and Love Are Inseparable
Dissolve Your Ties To Time
Gardens For The Future Future
Gardens For The Future Future

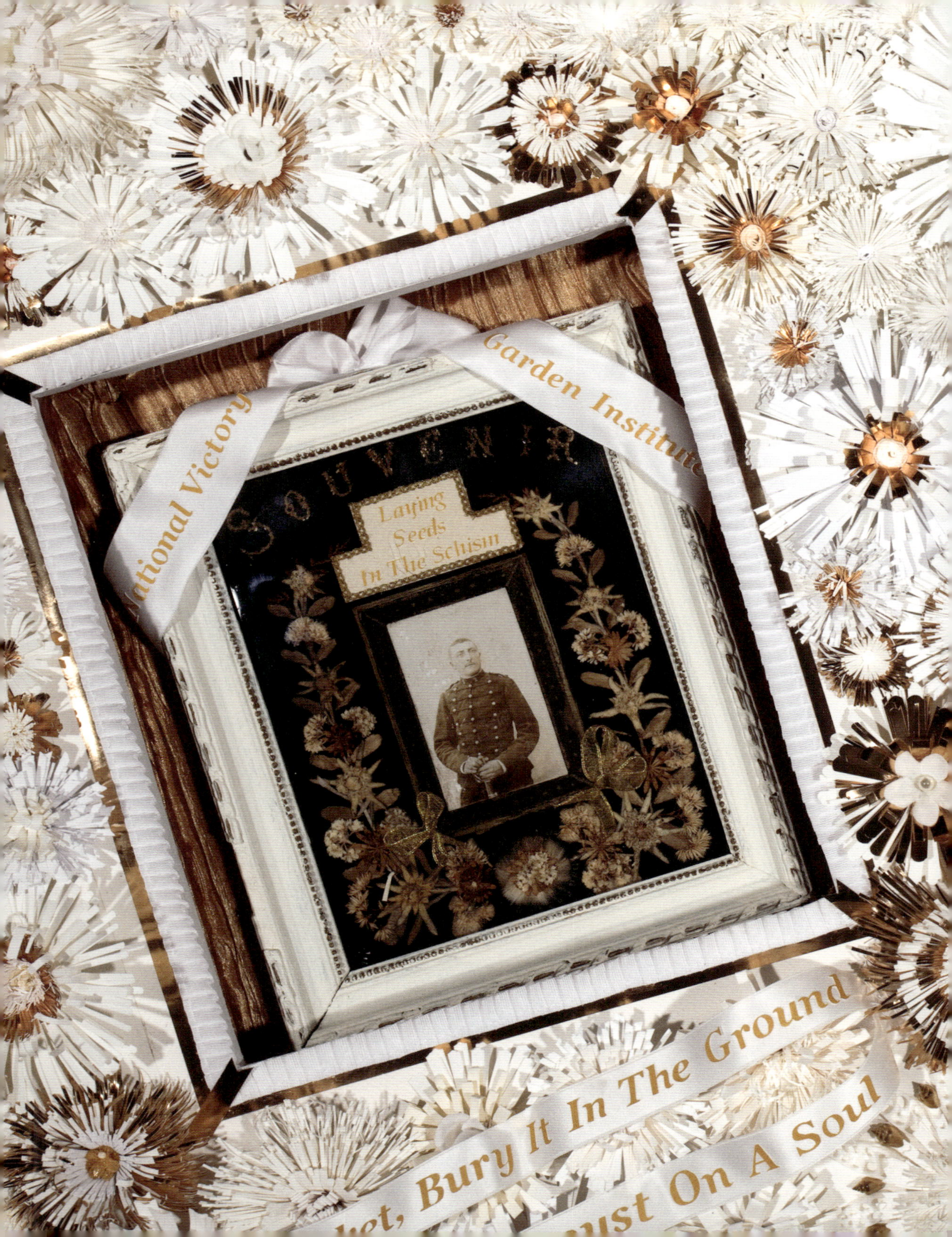

National Victory
Garden Institute
SOUVENIR
Laying Seeds In The Schism
Bury It In The Ground
Dust On A Soul

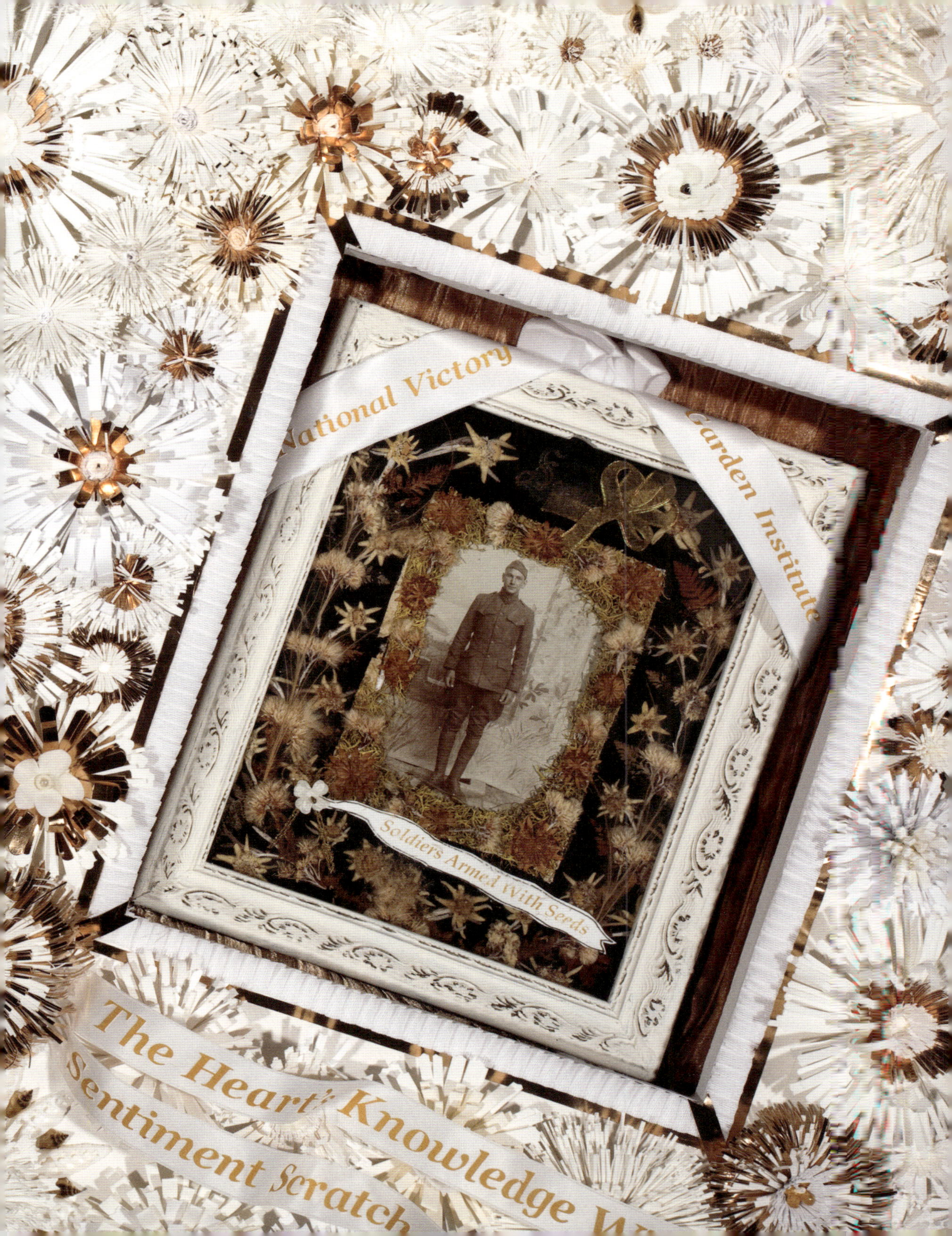

National Victory
Garden Institute
Soldiers Armed With Seeds
The Heart' Knowledge
Sentiment Scratch

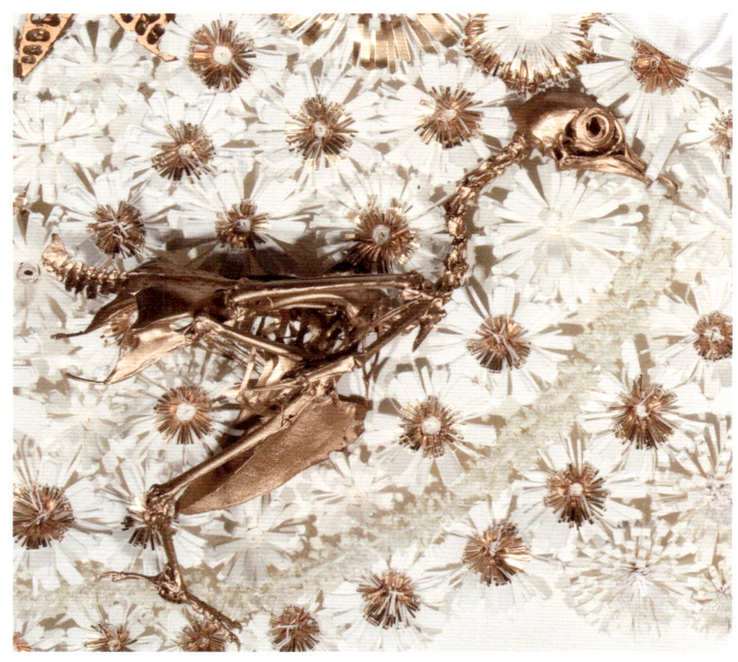

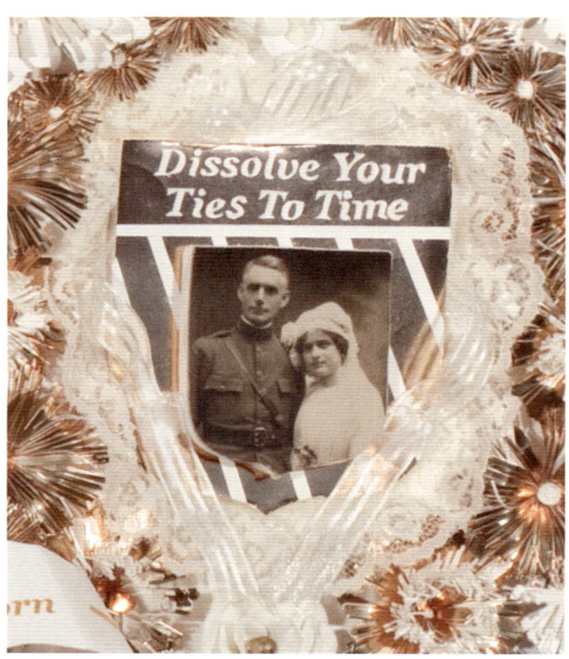
Dissolve Your
Ties To Time

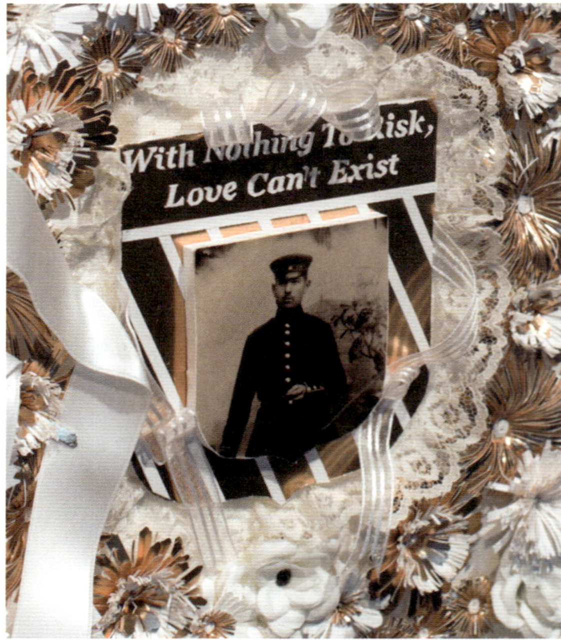
With Nothing To Risk,
Love Can't Exist

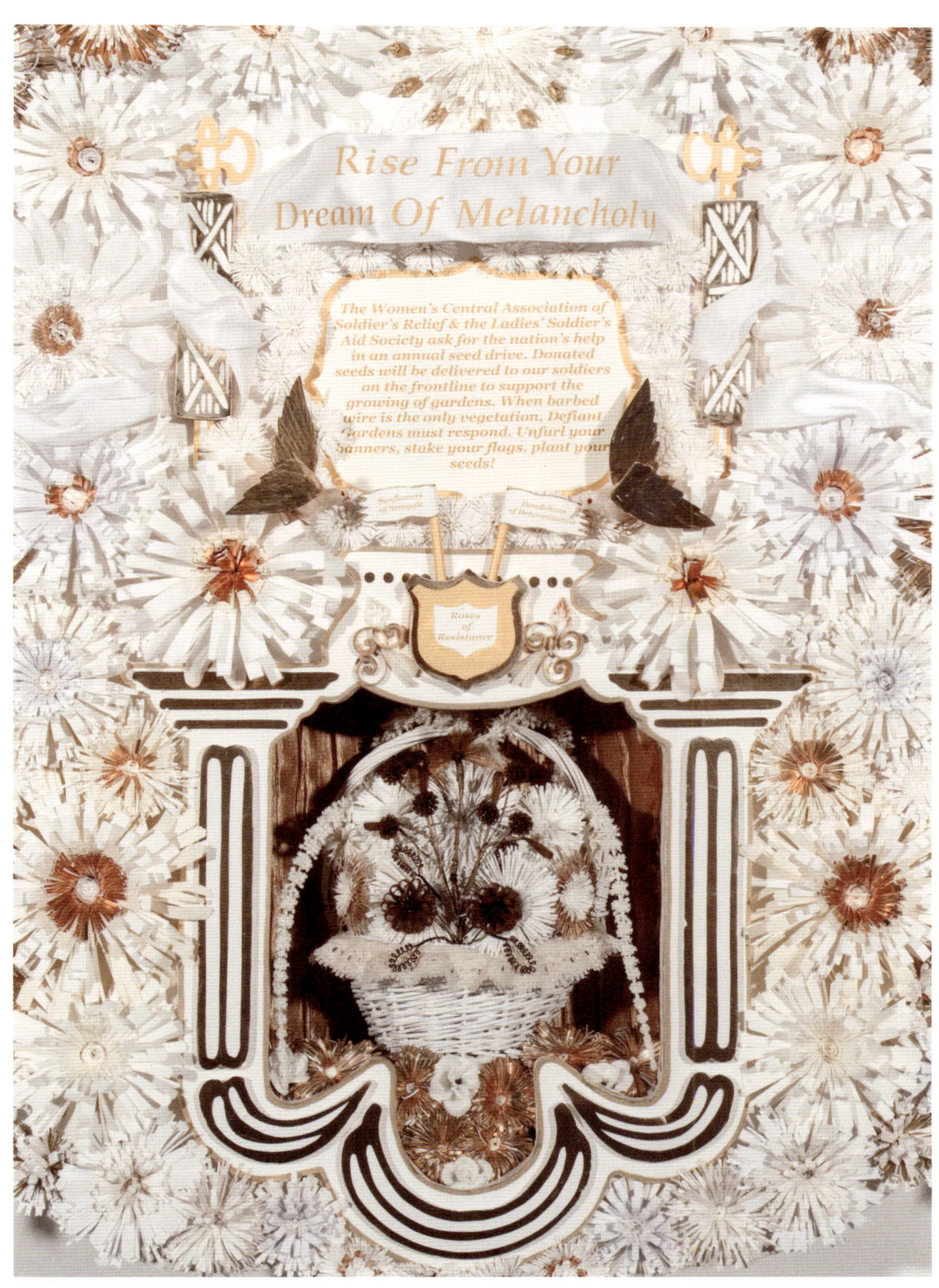

Rise From Your
Dream Of Melancholy

The Women's Central Association of
Soldier's Relief & the Ladies' Soldier's
Aid Society ask for the nation's help
in an annual seed drive. Donated
seeds will be delivered to our soldiers
on the frontline to support the
growing of gardens. When barbed
wire is the only vegetation, Defiant
Gardens must respond. Unfurl your
banners, stake your flags, plant your
seeds!

Sunflowers
of Strength

Dandelions of
Determination

Roses
of
Resistance

THE BOUNDARY OF
LIFE IS QUIETLY CROSSED

2008

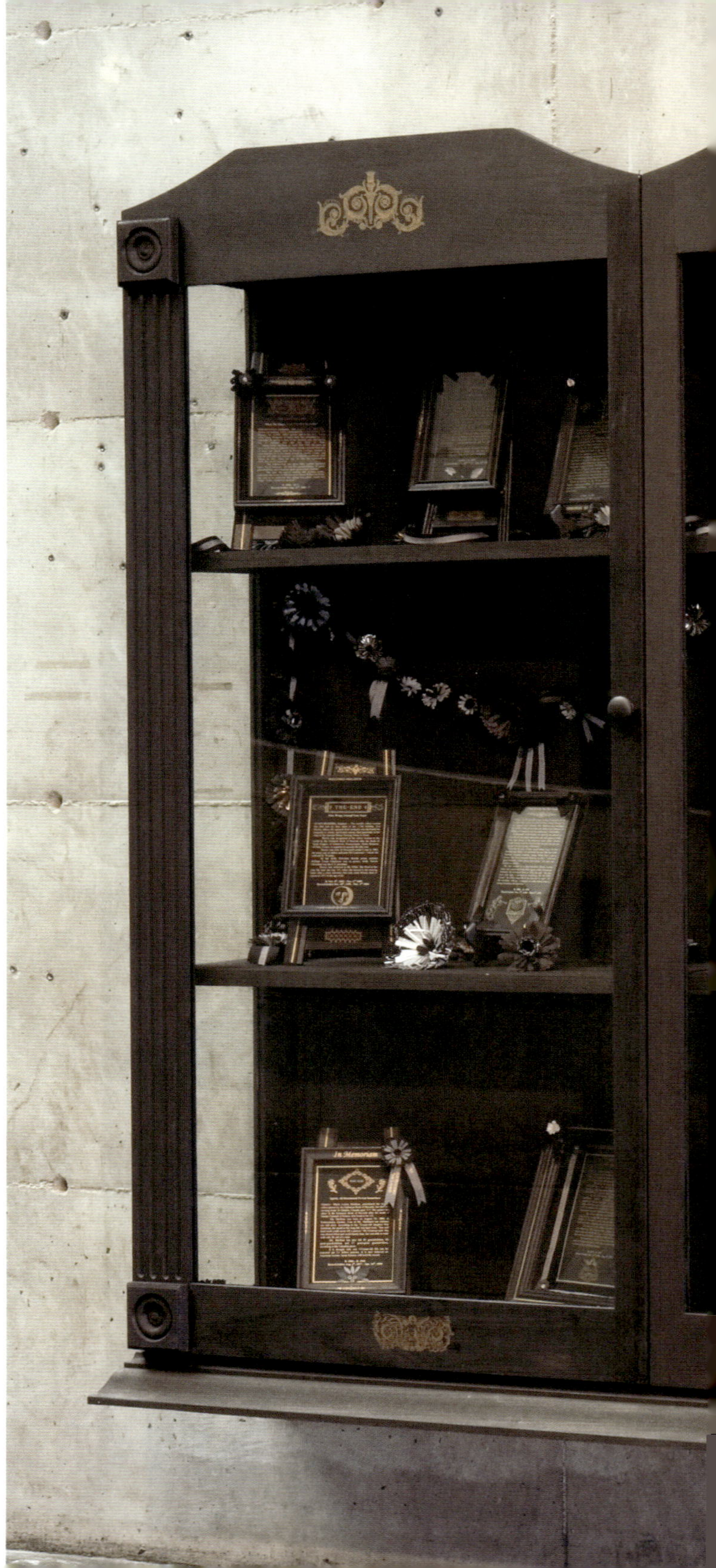

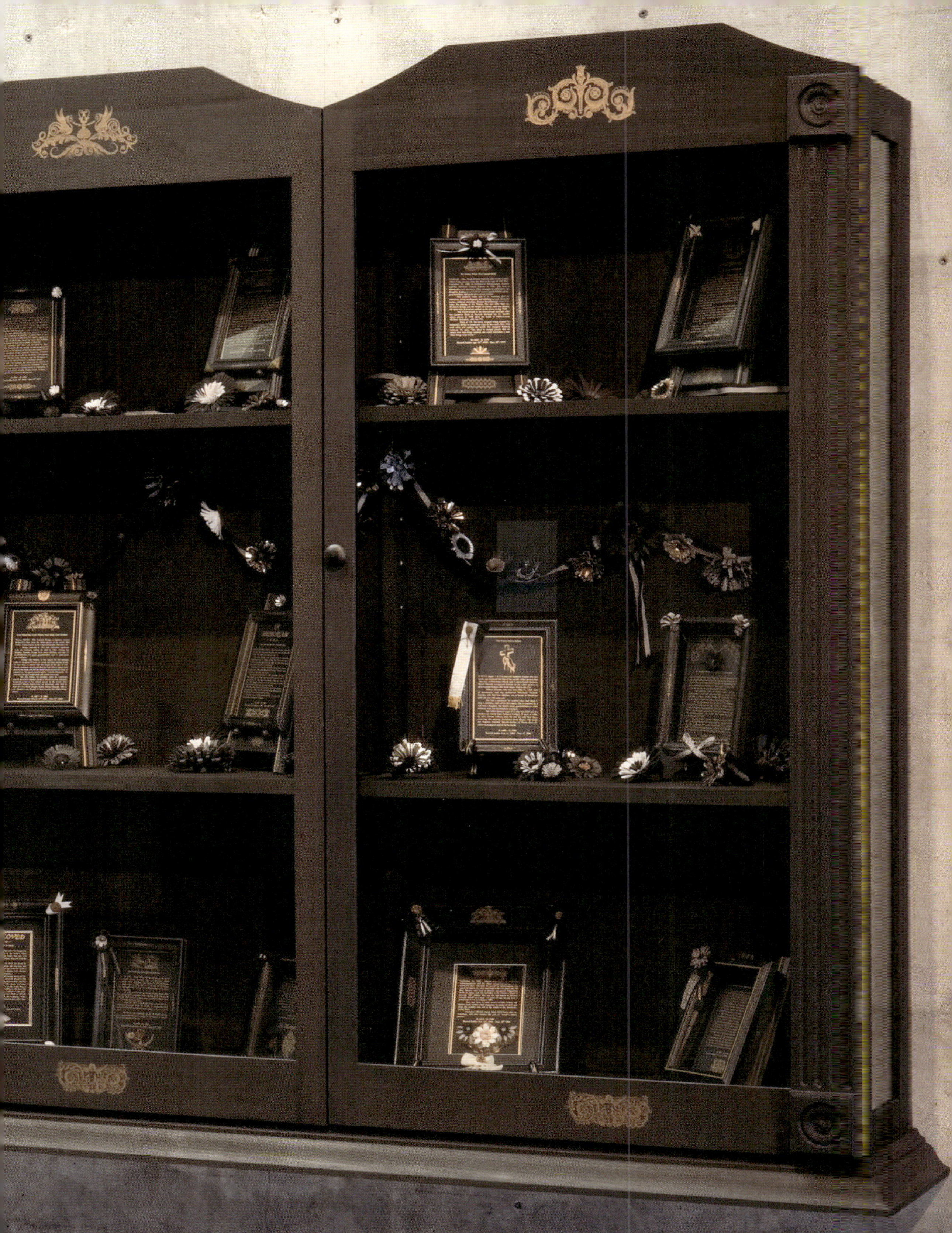

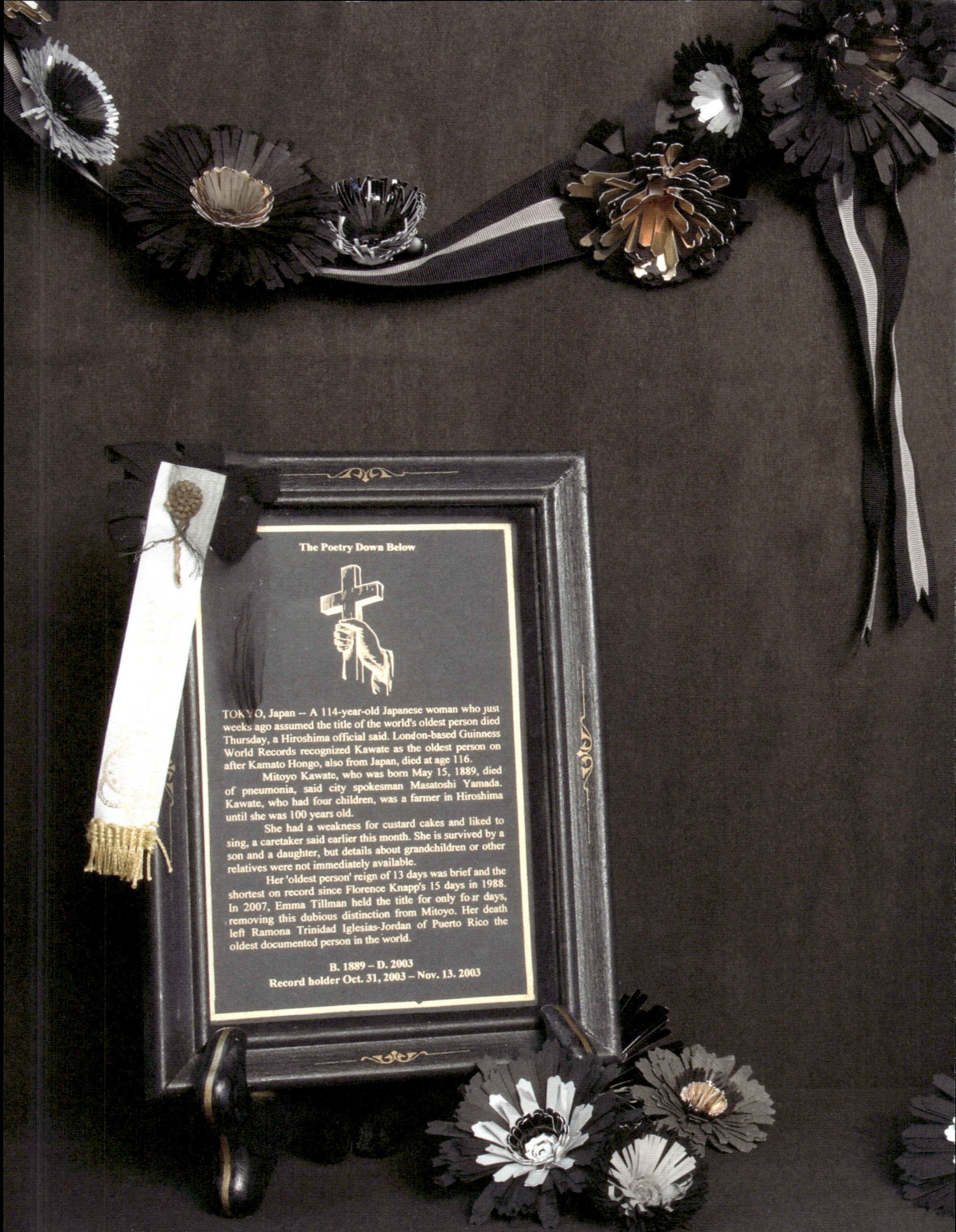

The Poetry Down Below

TOKYO, Japan -- A 114-year-old Japanese woman who just weeks ago assumed the title of the world's oldest person died Thursday, a London official said. London-based Guinness World Records recognized Kawate as the oldest person on after Kamato Hongo, also from Japan, died at age 116.

Mitoyo Kawate, who was born May 15, 1889, died of pneumonia, said city spokesman Masatoshi Yamada. Kawate, who had four children, was a farmer in Hiroshima until she was 100 years old.

She had a weakness for custard cakes and liked to sing, a caretaker said earlier this month. She is survived by a son and a daughter, but details about grandchildren or other relatives were not immediately available.

Her 'oldest person' reign of 13 days was brief and the shortest on record since Florence Knapp's 15 days in 1988. In 2007, Emma Tillman held the title for only four days, removing this dubious distinction from Mitoyo. Her death left Ramona Trinidad Iglesias-Jordan of Puerto Rico the oldest documented person in the world.

B. 1889 – D. 2003
Record holder Oct. 31, 2003 – Nov. 13. 2003

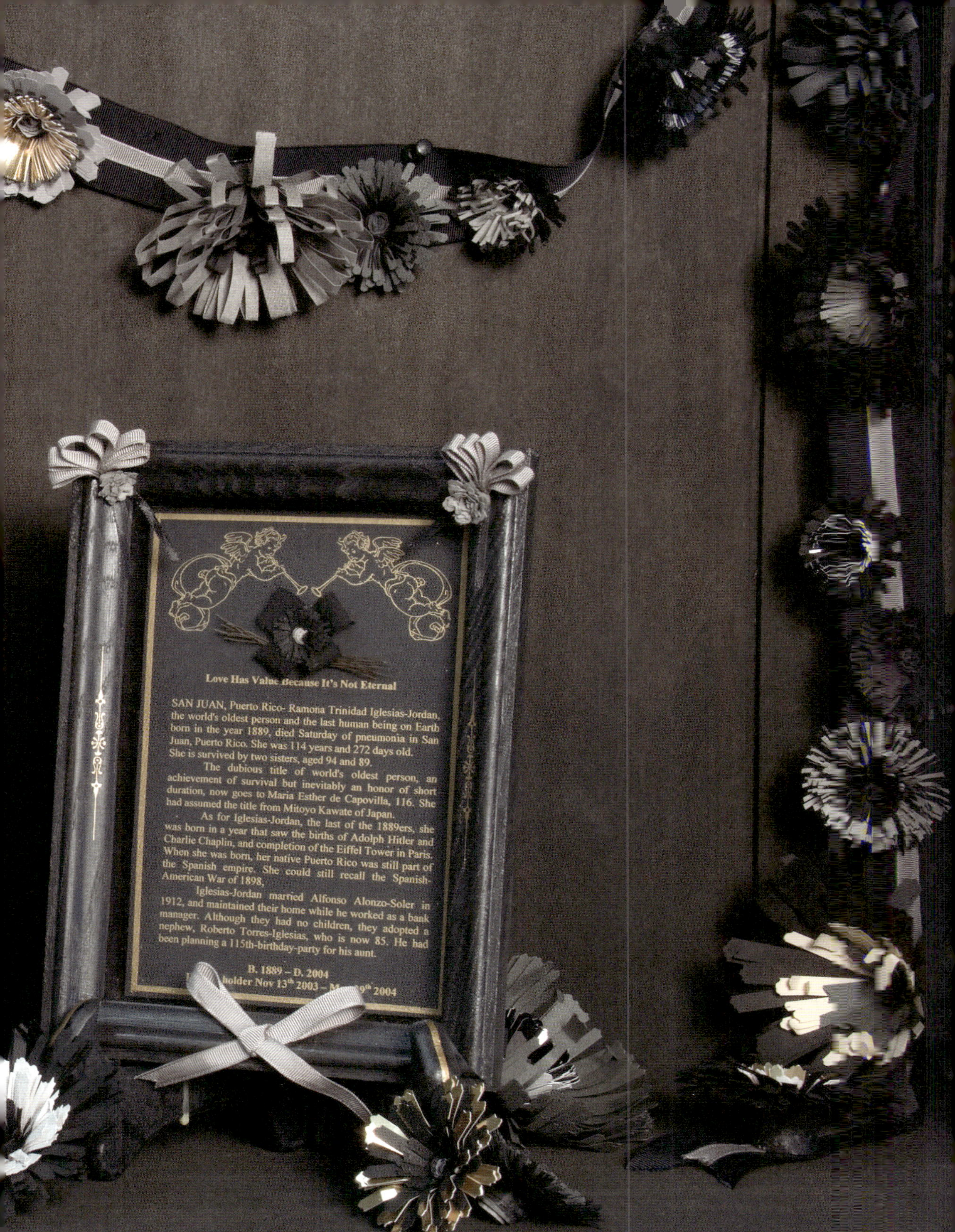

Love Has Value Because It's Not Eternal

SAN JUAN, Puerto Rico- Ramona Trinidad Iglesias-Jordan, the world's oldest person and the last human being on Earth born in the year 1889, died Saturday of pneumonia in San Juan, Puerto Rico. She was 114 years and 272 days old. She is survived by two sisters, aged 94 and 89.

The dubious title of world's oldest person, an achievement of survival but inevitably an honor of short duration, now goes to Maria Esther de Capovilla, 116. She had assumed the title from Mitoyo Kawate of Japan.

As for Iglesias-Jordan, the last of the 1889ers, she was born in a year that saw the births of Adolph Hitler and Charlie Chaplin, and completion of the Eiffel Tower in Paris. When she was born, her native Puerto Rico was still part of the Spanish empire. She could still recall the Spanish-American War of 1898,

Iglesias-Jordan married Alfonso Alonzo-Soler in 1912, and maintained their home while he worked as a bank manager. Although they had no children, they adopted a nephew, Roberto Torres-Iglesias, who is now 85. He had been planning a 115th-birthday-party for his aunt.

B. 1889 – D. 2004
holder Nov 13th 2003 – M   9th 2004

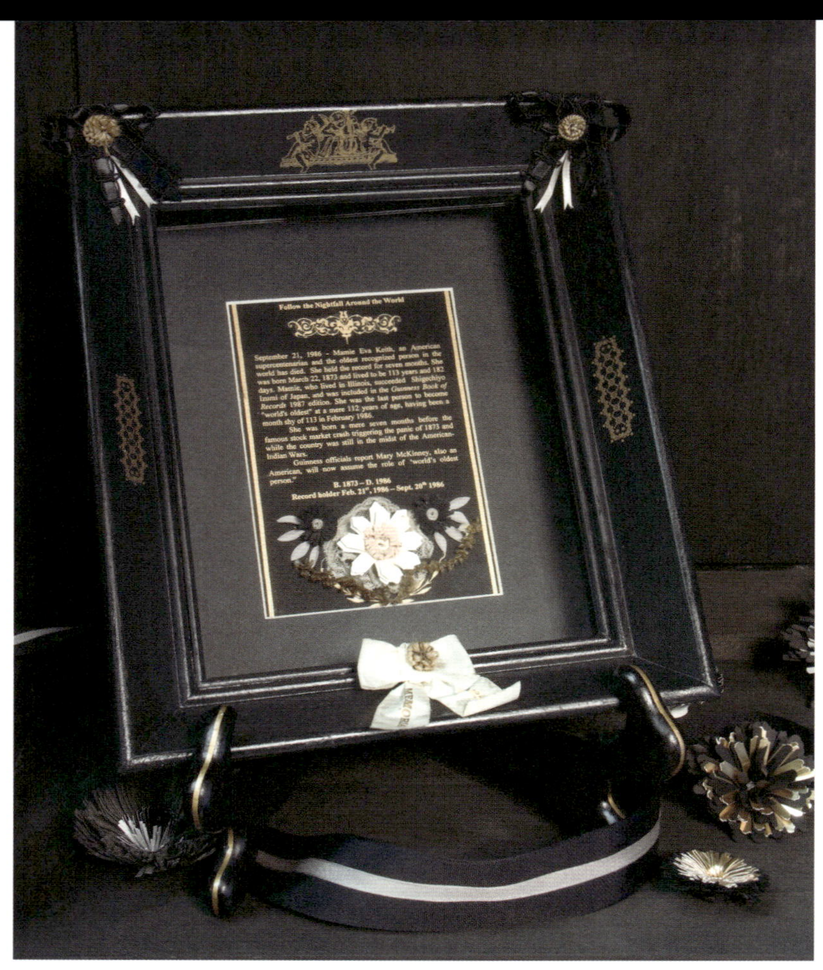

THE BOUNDARY OF LIFE IS QUIETLY CROSSED 2008

Ink-dyed poplar, typeset on cardstock, hair lockets made
of stretched and curled audiotape recordings
of supercentenarians (humans living to 110 or older),
19th-century hair flowers, lace and fabric from widows' mourning
dresses, colored paper, silk, antique ribbon, homemade paper,
willow, ash, white oak, milk paint, glass

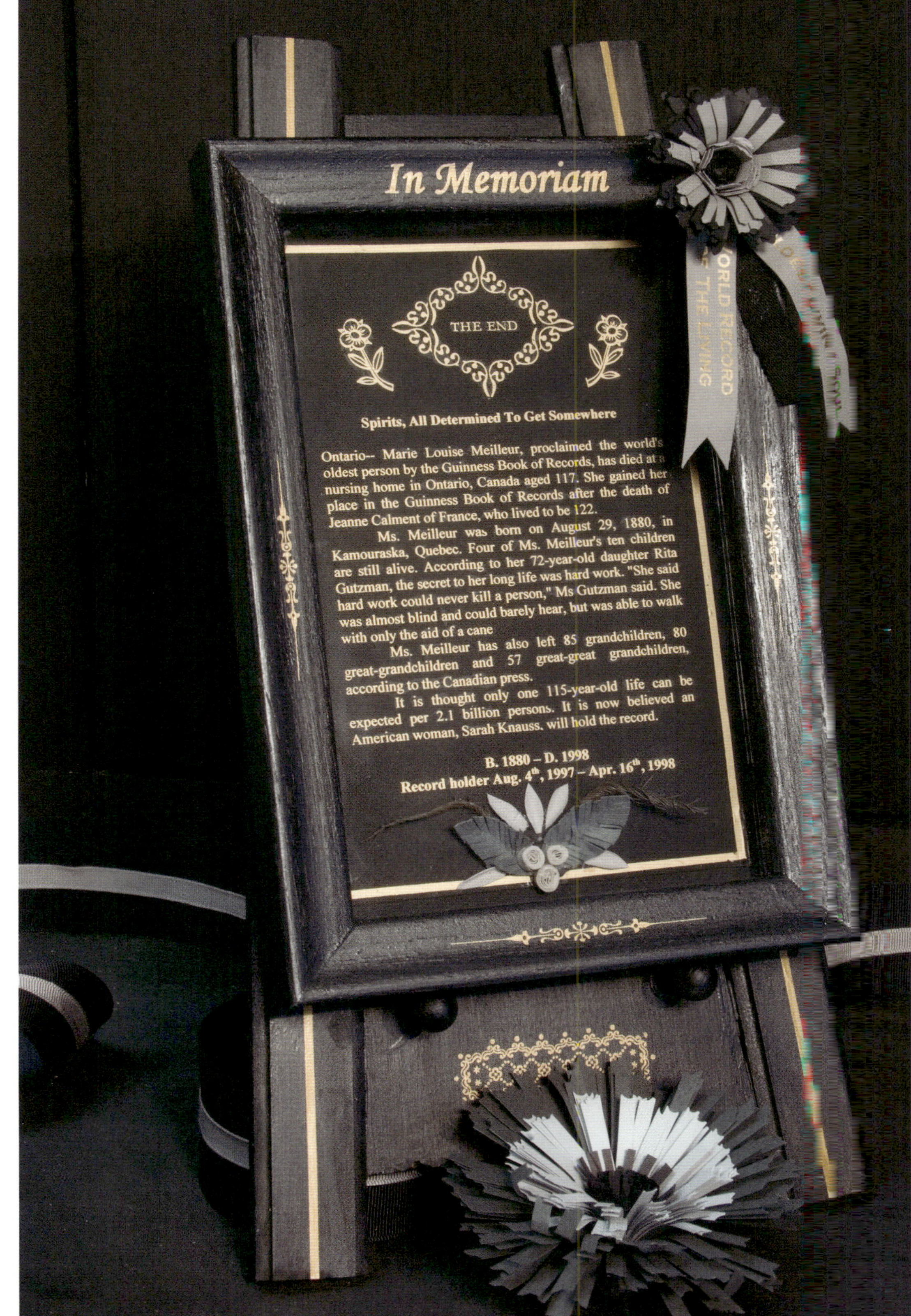
In Memoriam
THE END
Spirits, All Determined To Get Somewhere

Ontario-- Marie Louise Meilleur, proclaimed the world's oldest person by the Guinness Book of Records, has died at a nursing home in Ontario, Canada aged 117. She gained her place in the Guinness Book of Records after the death of Jeanne Calment of France, who lived to be 122.
Ms. Meilleur was born on August 29, 1880, in Kamouraska, Quebec. Four of Ms. Meilleur's ten children are still alive. According to her 72-year-old daughter Rita Gutzman, the secret to her long life was hard work. "She said hard work could never kill a person," Ms Gutzman said. She was almost blind and could barely hear, but was able to walk with only the aid of a cane
Ms. Meilleur has also left 85 grandchildren, 80 great-grandchildren and 57 great-great grandchildren, according to the Canadian press.
It is thought only one 115-year-old life can be expected per 2.1 billion persons. It is now believed an American woman, Sarah Knauss, will hold the record.

B. 1880 – D. 1998
Record holder Aug. 4th, 1997 – Apr. 16th, 1998

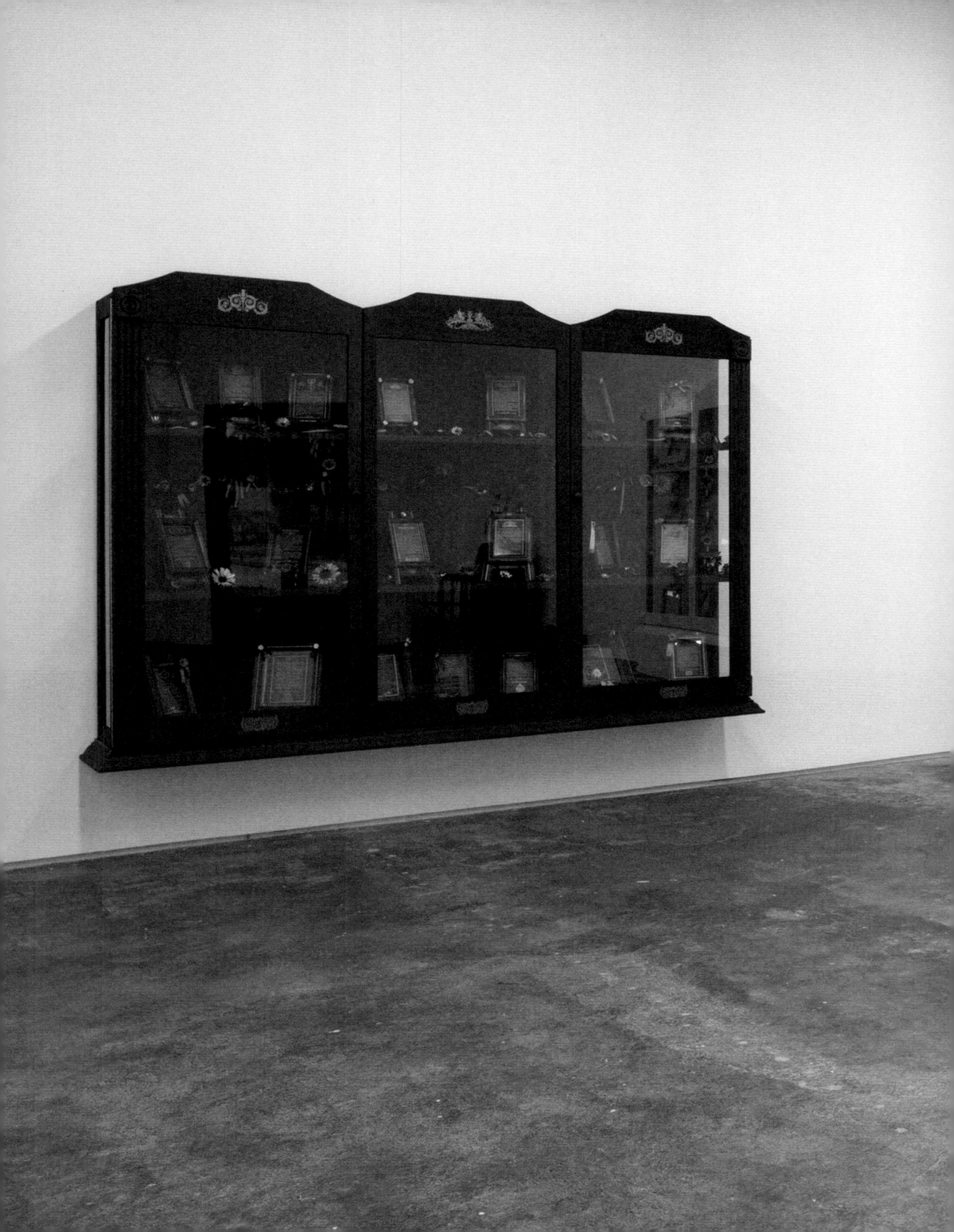

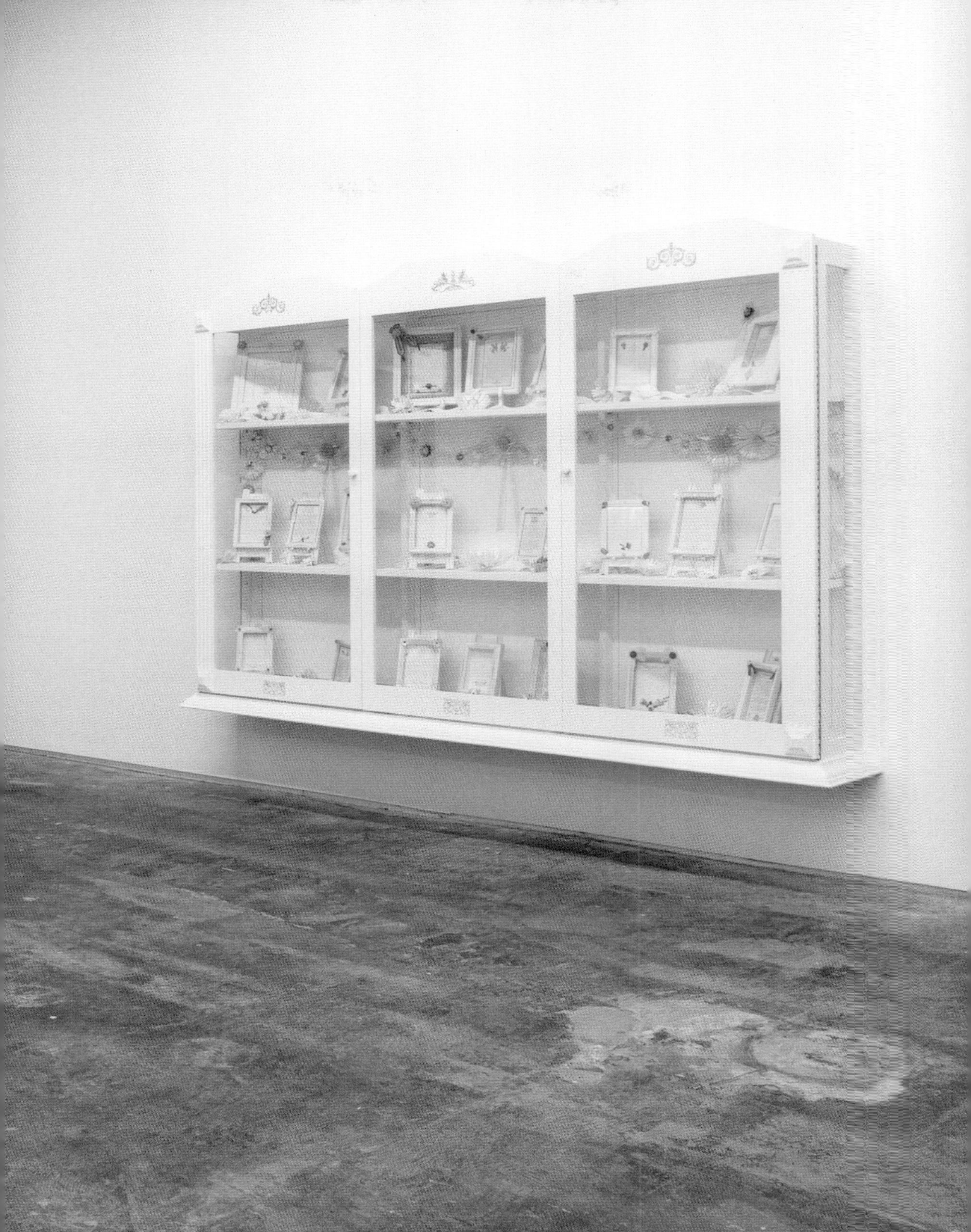

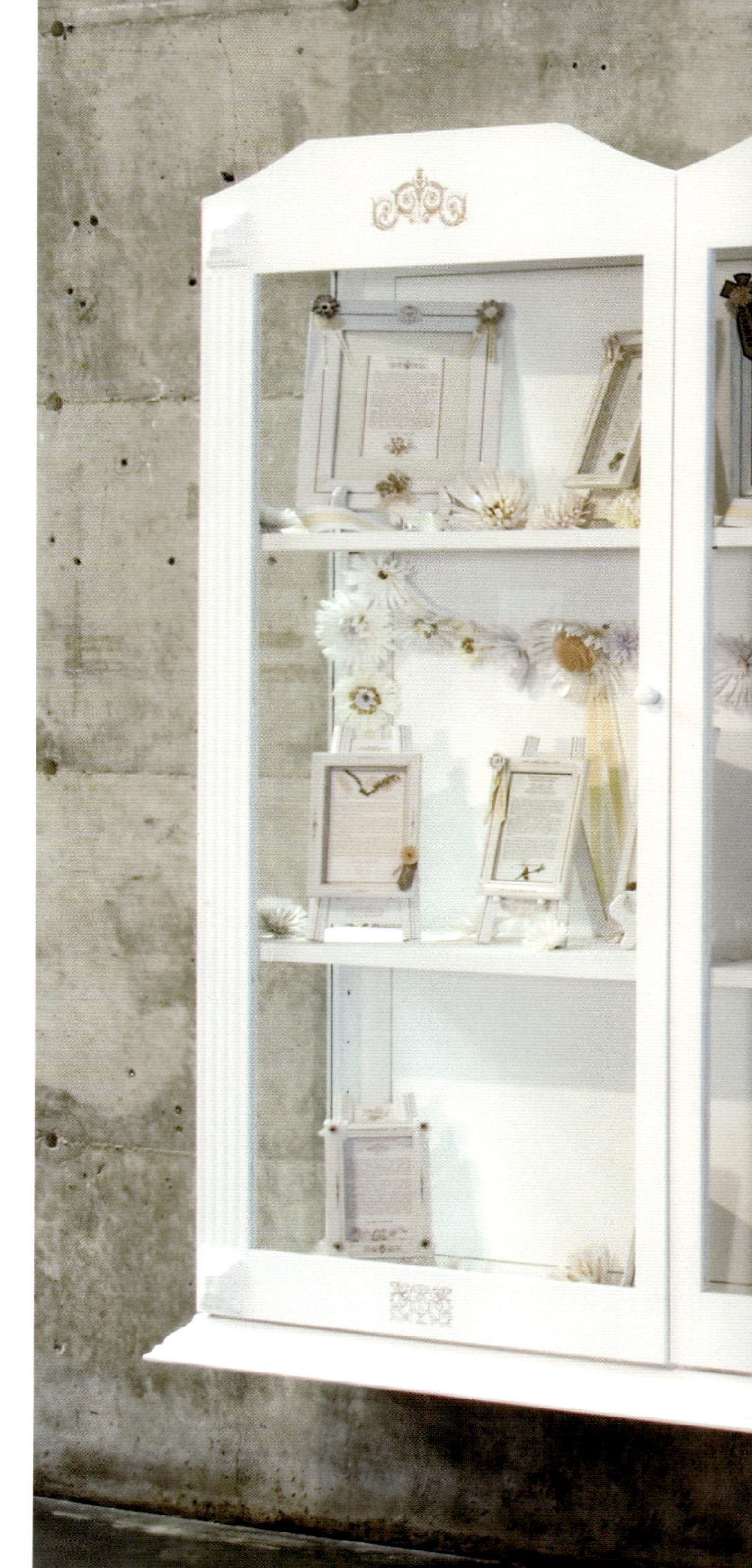

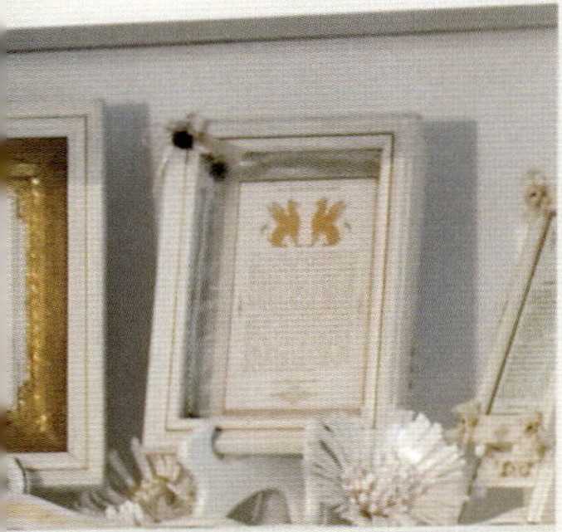
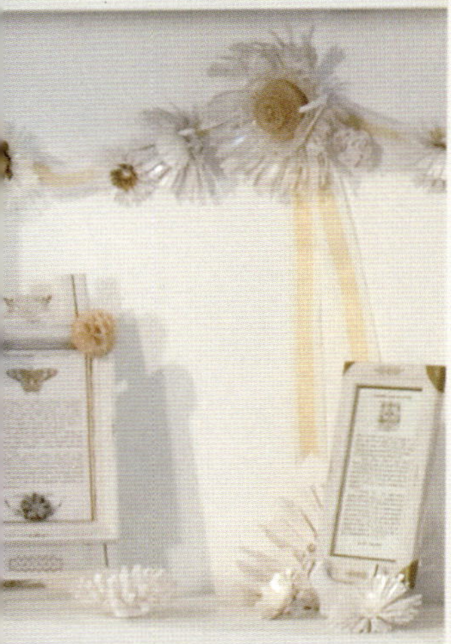

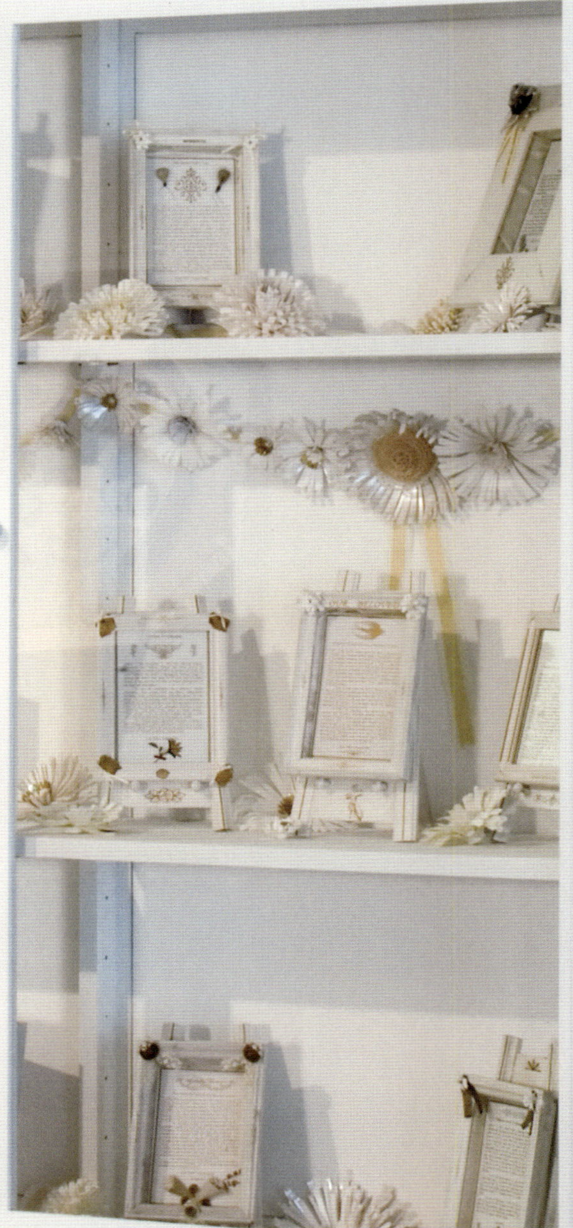

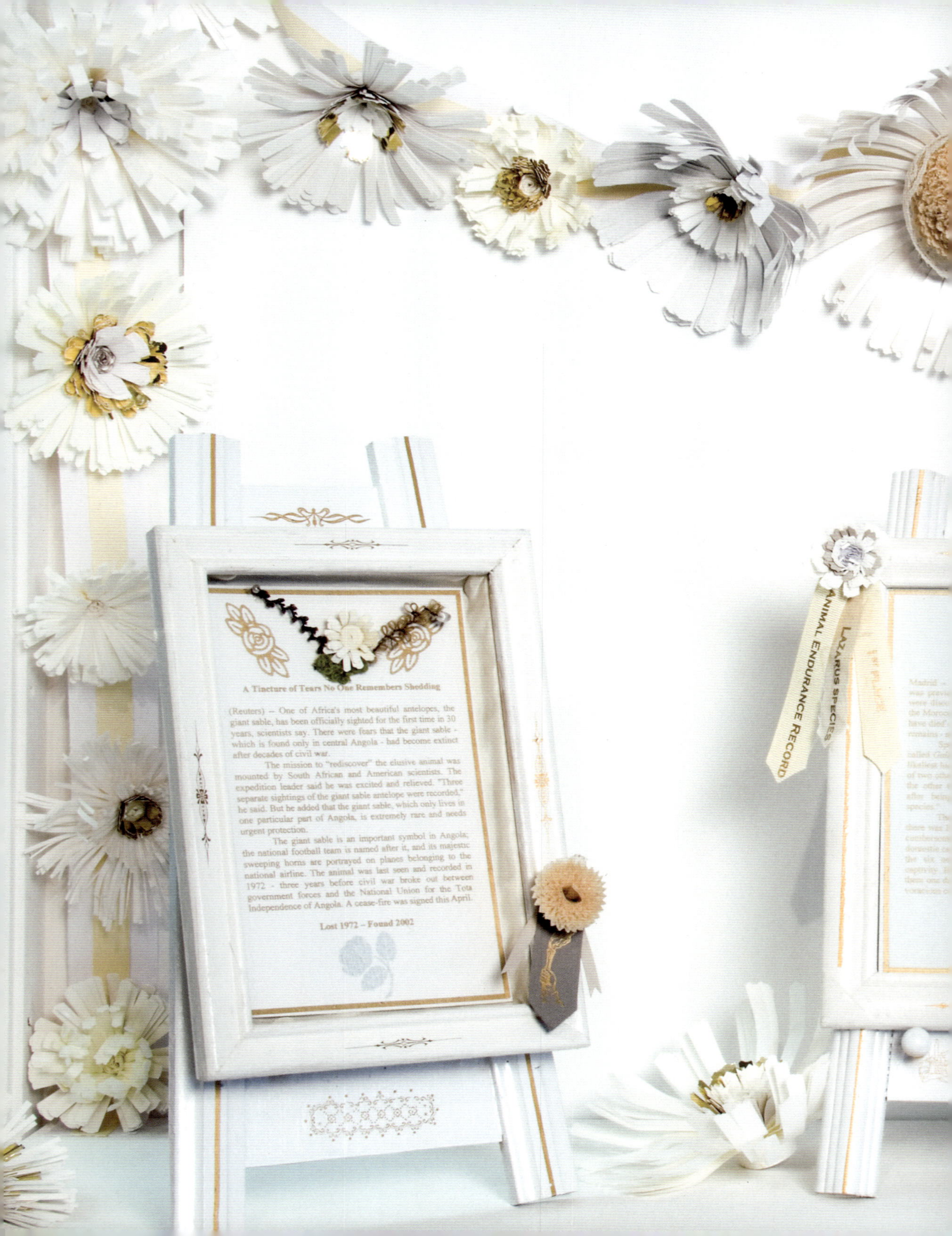

A Tincture of Tears No One Remembers Shedding

(Reuters) — One of Africa's most beautiful antelopes, the giant sable, has been officially sighted for the first time in 30 years, scientists say. There were fears that the giant sable - which is found only in central Angola - had become extinct after decades of civil war.

The mission to "rediscover" the elusive animal was mounted by South African and American scientists. The expedition leader said he was excited and relieved. "Three separate sightings of the giant sable antelope were recorded," he said. But he added that the giant sable, which only lives in one particular part of Angola, is extremely rare and needs urgent protection.

The giant sable is an important symbol in Angola; the national football team is named after it, and its majestic sweeping horns are portrayed on planes belonging to the national airline. The animal was last seen and recorded in 1972 - three years before civil war broke out between government forces and the National Union for the Total Independence of Angola. A cease-fire was signed this April.

Lost 1972 – Found 2002

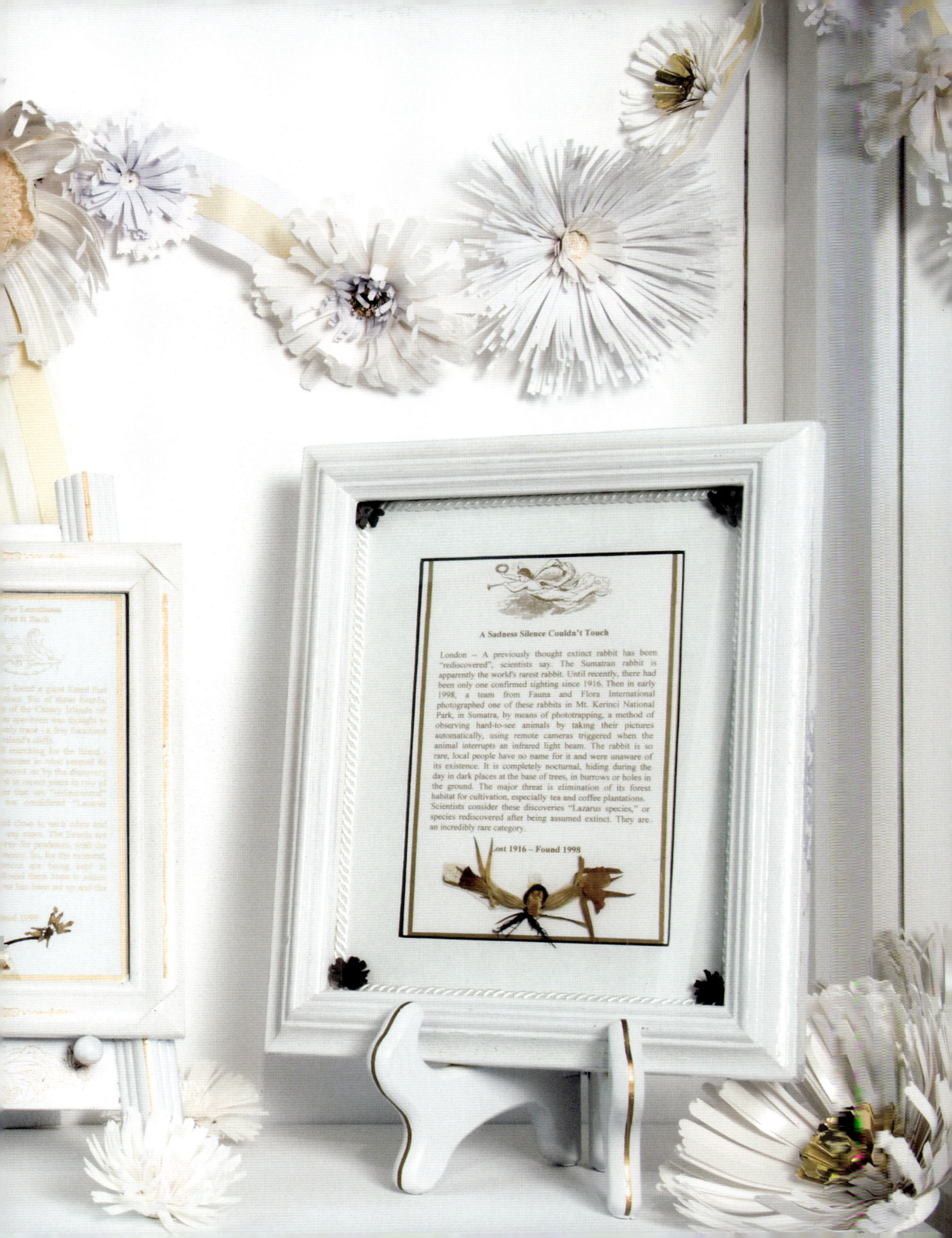

A Sadness Silence Couldn't Touch

London — A previously thought extinct rabbit has been "rediscovered", scientists say. The Sumatran rabbit is apparently the world's rarest rabbit. Until recently, there had been only one confirmed sighting since 1916. Then in early 1998, a team from Fauna and Flora International photographed one of these rabbits in Mt. Kerinci National Park, in Sumatra, by means of phototrapping, a method of observing hard-to-see animals by taking their pictures automatically, using remote cameras triggered when the animal interrupts an infrared light beam. The rabbit is so rare, local people have no name for it and were unaware of its existence. It is completely nocturnal, hiding during the day in dark places at the base of trees, in burrows or holes in the ground. The major threat is elimination of its forest habitat for cultivation, especially tea and coffee plantations. Scientists consider these discoveries "Lazarus species," or species rediscovered after being assumed extinct. They are an incredibly rare category.

Lost 1916 — Found 1998

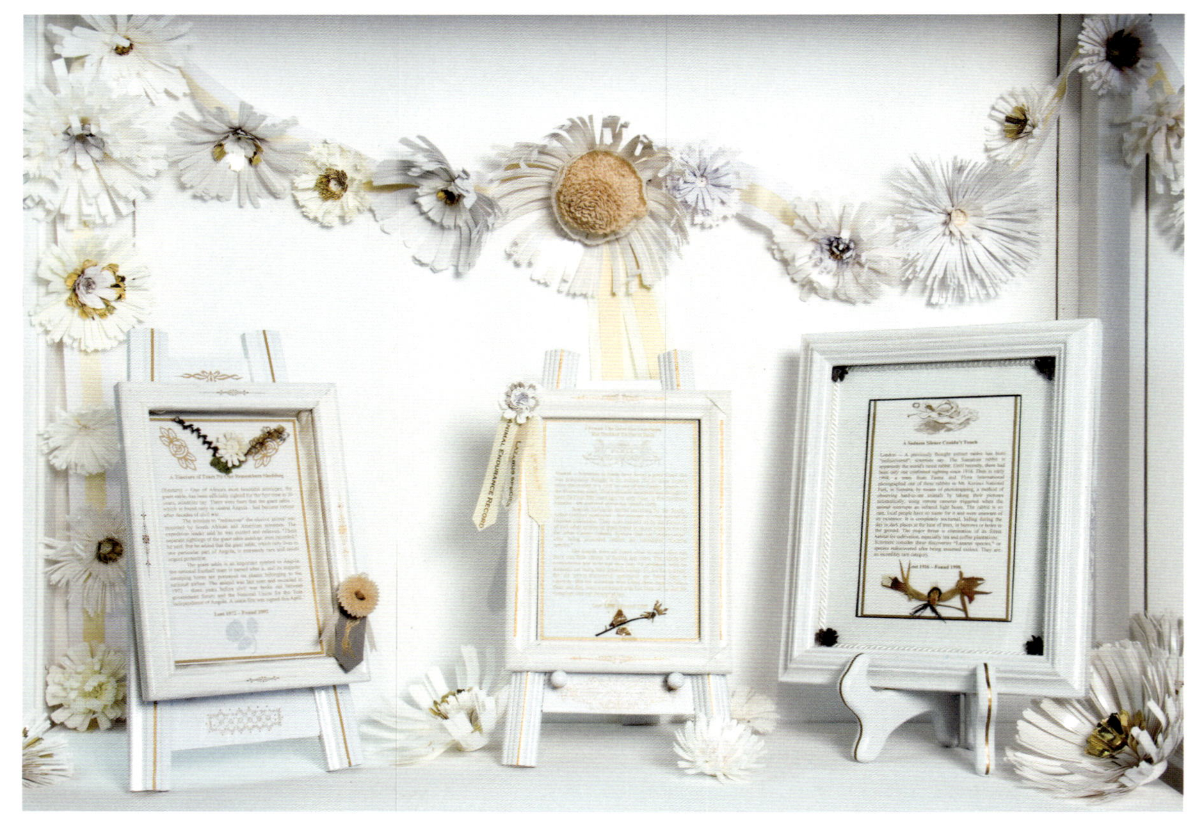

THE ARK OF FRAILTY 2008

Poplar, typeset on cardstock, hair lockets made of
stretched and curled audiotape recordings of "Lazarus species"
(species that are rediscovered alive after being classified extinct)
in the wild, 19th-century hair flowers, 19th-century dried flowers,
lace and fabric from widows' mourning dresses, colored paper, silk,
antique ribbon and buttons, carved animal bone buttons,
homemade paper, willow, ash, white oak, milk paint, glass

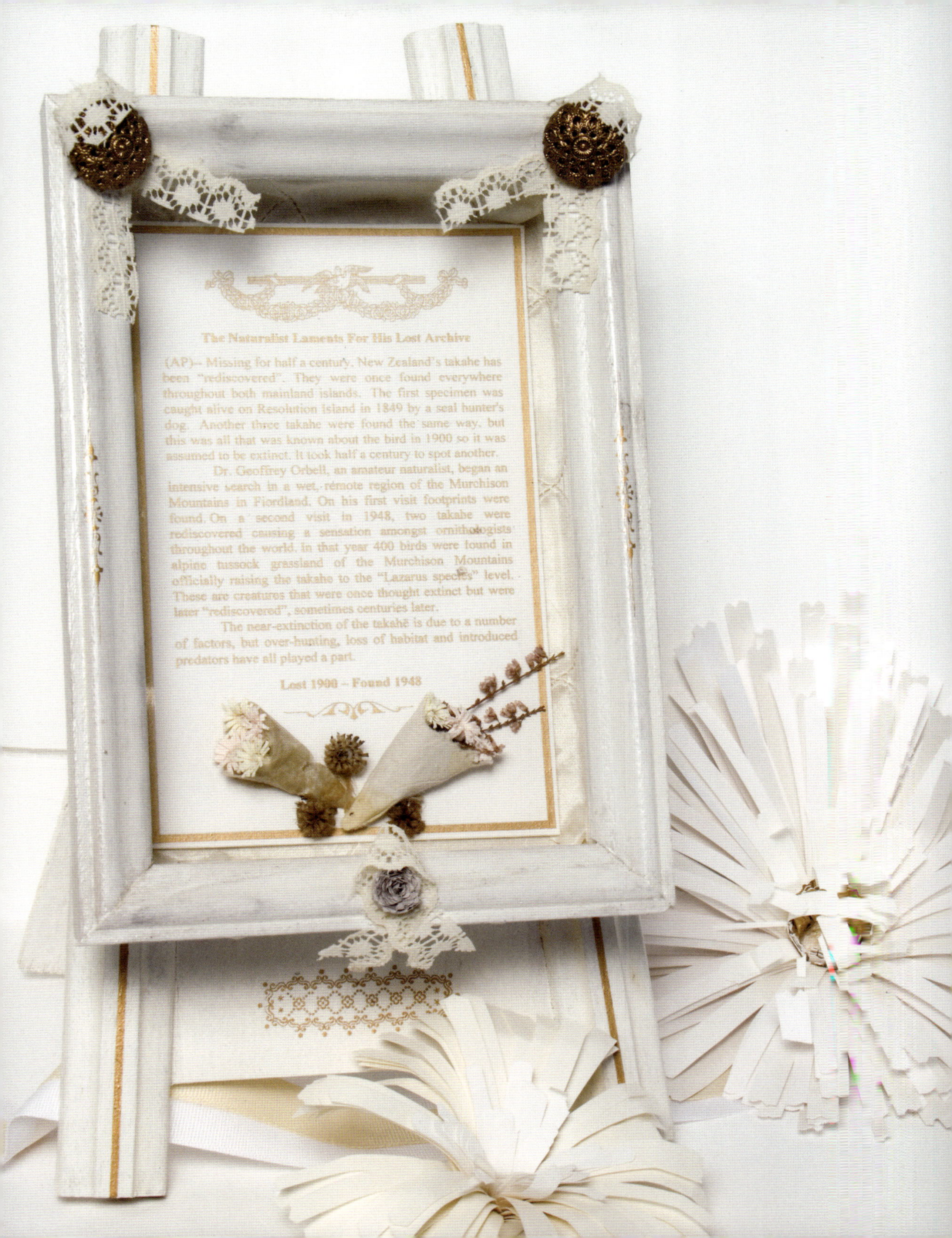

The Naturalist Laments For His Lost Archive

(AP)-- Missing for half a century, New Zealand's takahe has been "rediscovered". They were once found everywhere throughout both mainland islands. The first specimen was caught alive on Resolution Island in 1849 by a seal hunter's dog. Another three takahe were found the same way, but this was all that was known about the bird in 1900 so it was assumed to be extinct. It took half a century to spot another.

Dr. Geoffrey Orbell, an amateur naturalist, began an intensive search in a wet, remote region of the Murchison Mountains in Fiordland. On his first visit footprints were found. On a second visit in 1948, two takahe were rediscovered causing a sensation amongst ornithologists throughout the world. In that year 400 birds were found in alpine tussock grassland of the Murchison Mountains officially raising the takahe to the "Lazarus species" level. These are creatures that were once thought extinct but were later "rediscovered", sometimes centuries later.

The near-extinction of the takahē is due to a number of factors, but over-hunting, loss of habitat and introduced predators have all played a part.

Lost 1900 – Found 1948

SOME LONGINGS SURVIVE DEATH 2008

Glacially released 50,000-year old woolly mammoth tusks,
19th-century braided hair flowers of various lovers intertwined
with glacially released woolly mammoth hair, carved ivory
and bone, bocote, colored paper, silk, ribbon, typeset

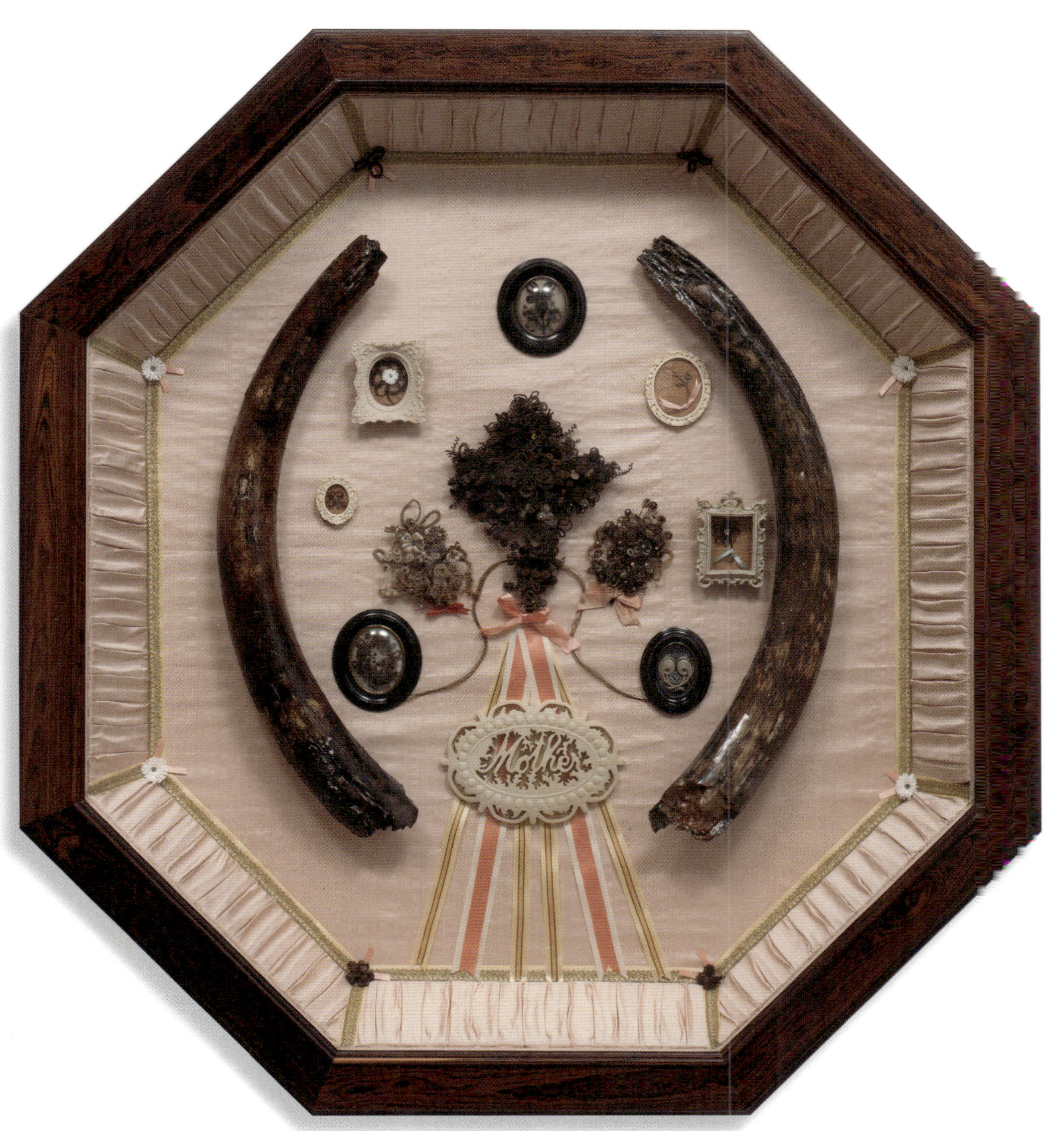

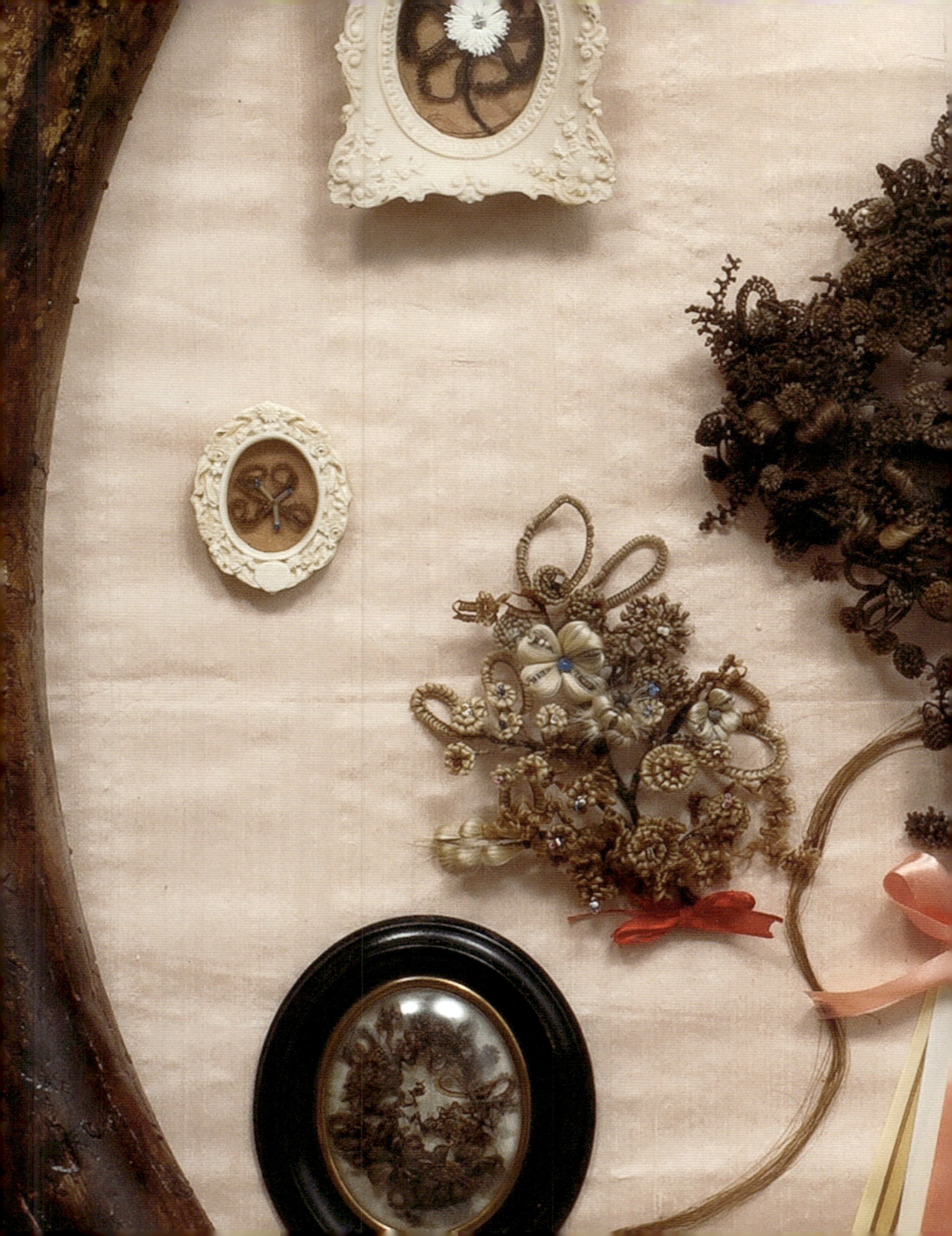

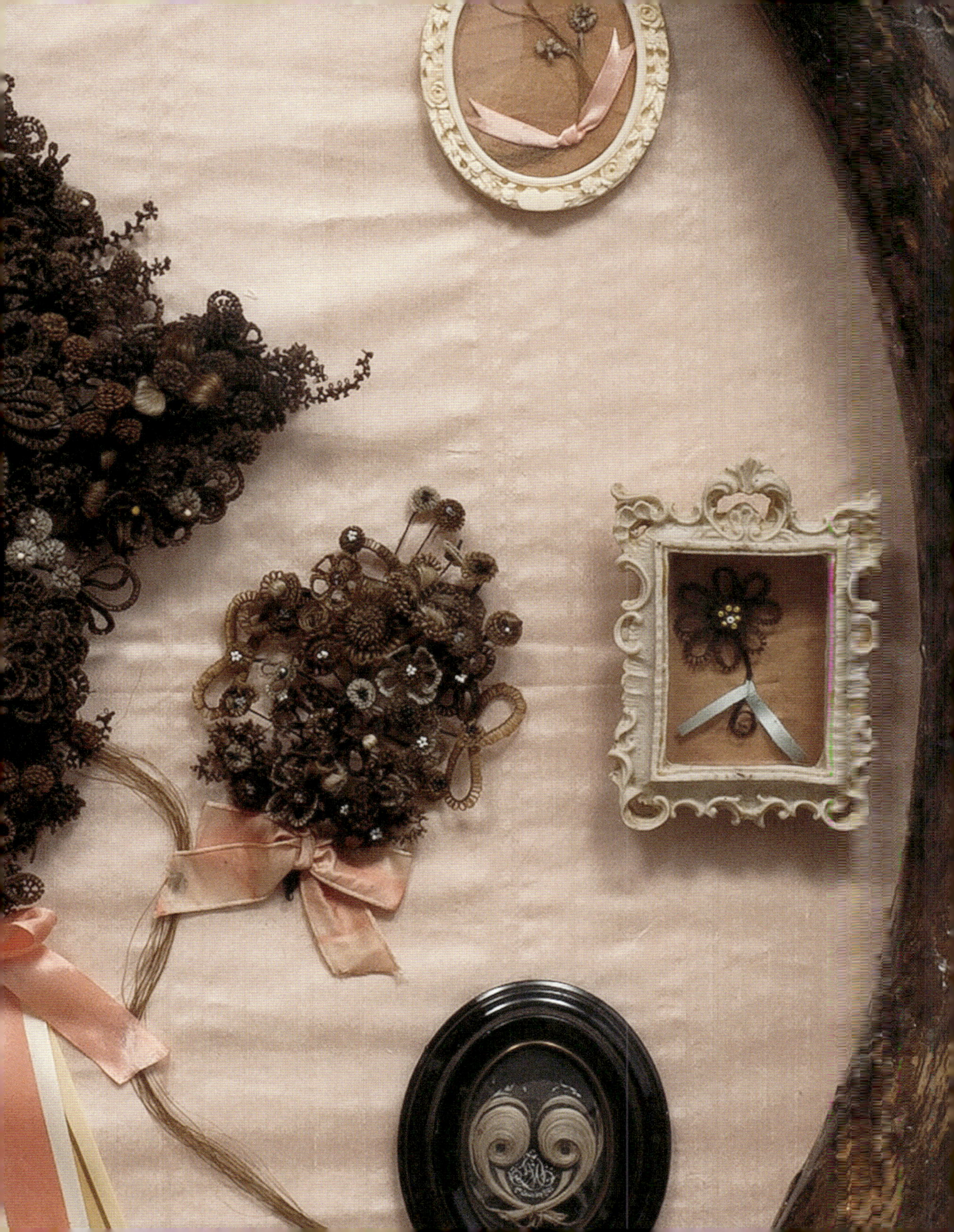

FOLKS ON THE FRINGE 2009

Cut paper, colored pencil, foam core, glue

MAIDENS OF MOTHER'S MILK THISTLE 2009

Cut paper, colored pencil, foam core, glue

ALCHEMICAL GARDENS 2009

Cut paper, colored pencil, foam core, glue

SOCIETY OF SEEKERS 2009

Cut paper, colored pencil, foam core, glue

A HOMEOPATHIC TREATMENT
FOR HUMAN LONGING

2008

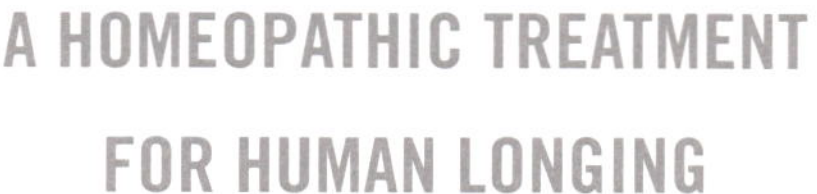

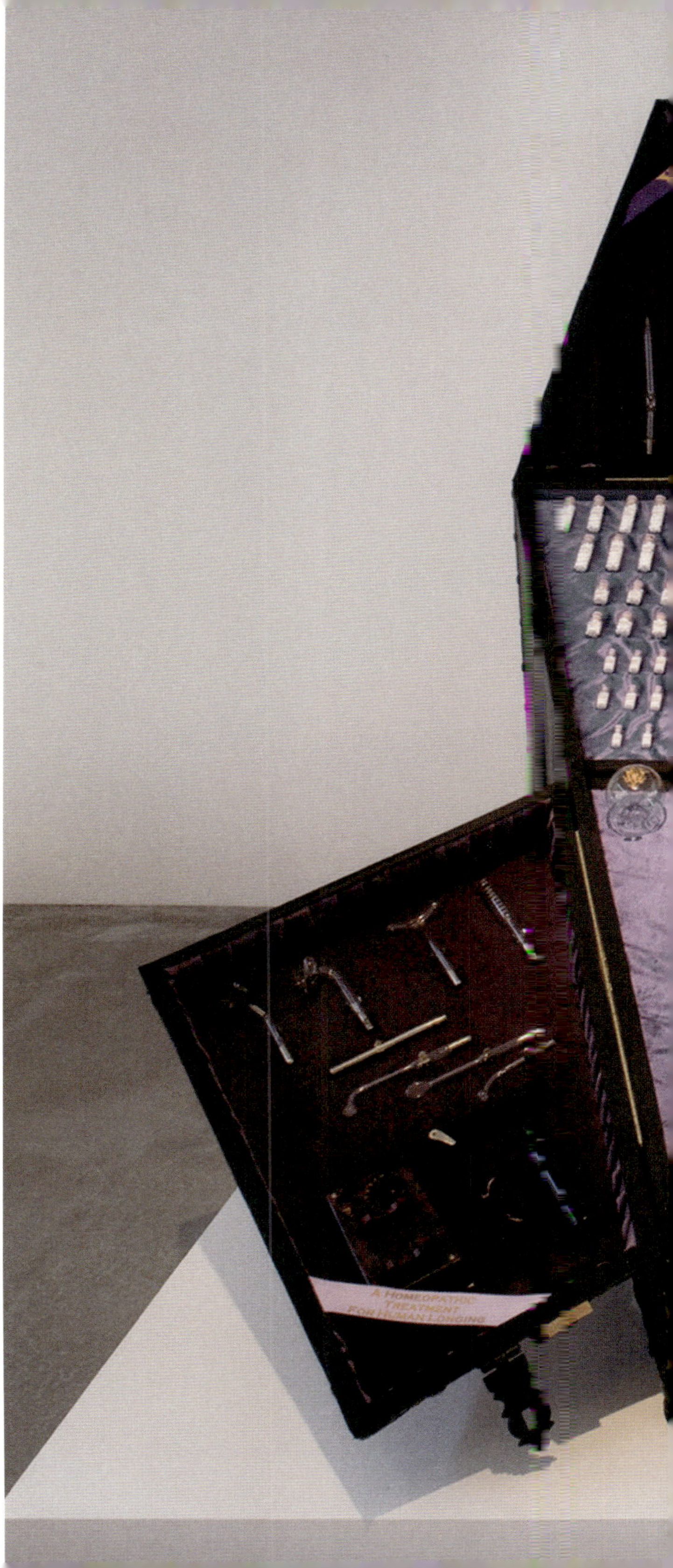

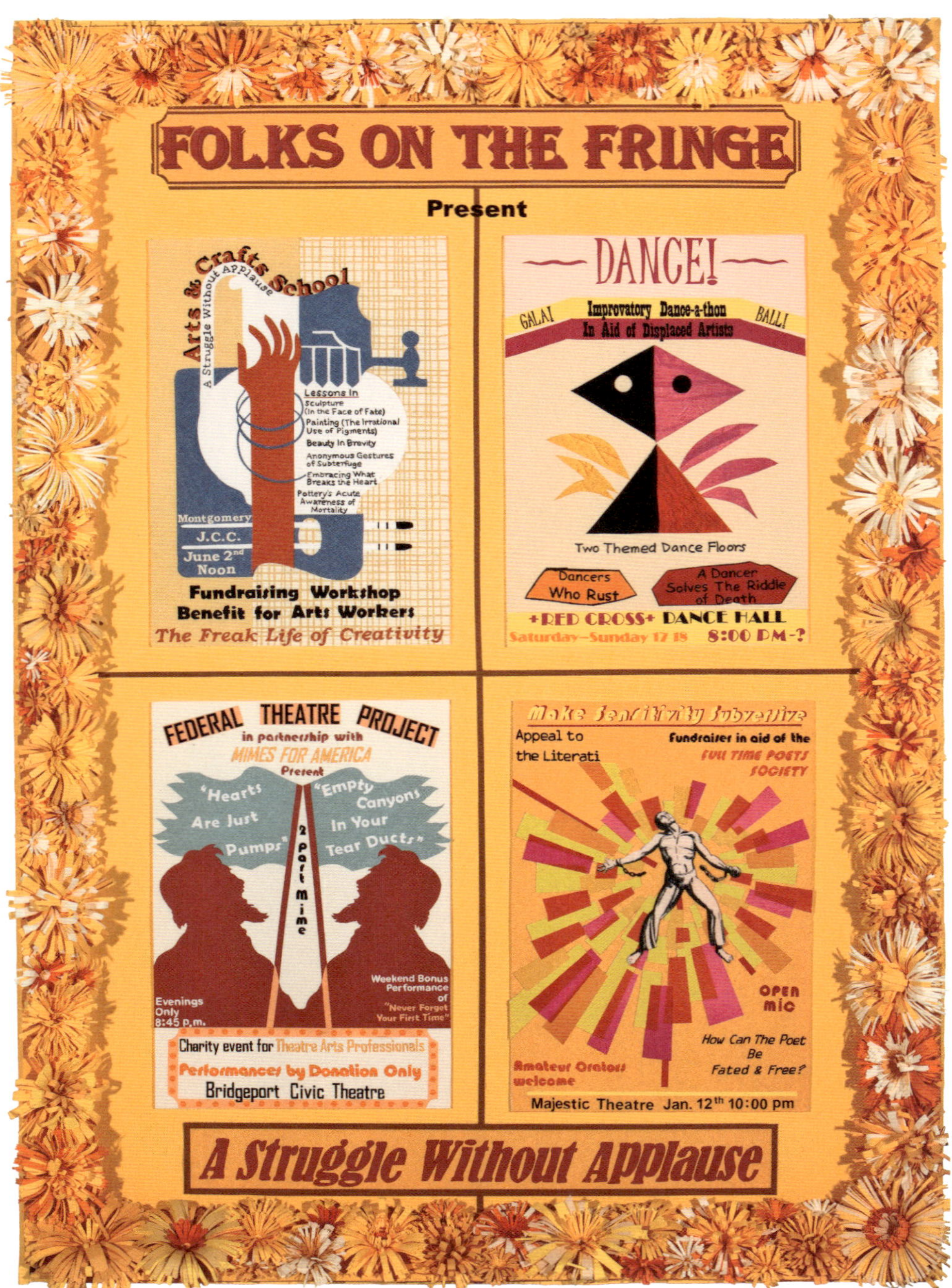

FOLKS ON THE FRINGE
Present

Arts & Crafts School
A Struggle Without Applause
Lessons In
Sculpture
(In the Face of Fate)
Painting (The Irrational Use of Pigments)
Beauty In Brevity
Anonymous Gestures of Subterfuge
Embracing What Breaks the Heart
Pottery's Acute Awareness of Mortality
Montgomery
J.C.C.
June 2nd
Noon
Fundraising Workshop
Benefit for Arts Workers
The Freak Life of Creativity

DANCE!
GALA!
BALL!
Improvatory Dance-a-thon
In Aid of Displaced Artists
Two Themed Dance Floors
Dancers Who Rust
A Dancer Solves The Riddle of Death
+RED CROSS+ DANCE HALL
Saturday—Sunday 17 18
8:00 PM-?

FEDERAL THEATRE PROJECT
in partnership with
MIMES FOR AMERICA
Present
"Hearts Are Just Pumps"
"Empty Canyons In Your Tear Ducts"
2 Part mime
Evenings Only
8:45 p.m.
Weekend Bonus Performance of "Never Forget Your First Time"
Charity event for Theatre Arts Professionals
Performances by Donation Only
Bridgeport Civic Theatre

Make Sensitivity Subvertize
Appeal to the Literati
Fundraiser in aid of the
FULL TIME POETS SOCIETY
OPEN mic
How Can The Poet Be Fated & Free?
Amateur Orators welcome
Majestic Theatre Jan. 12th 10:00 pm

A Struggle Without Applause

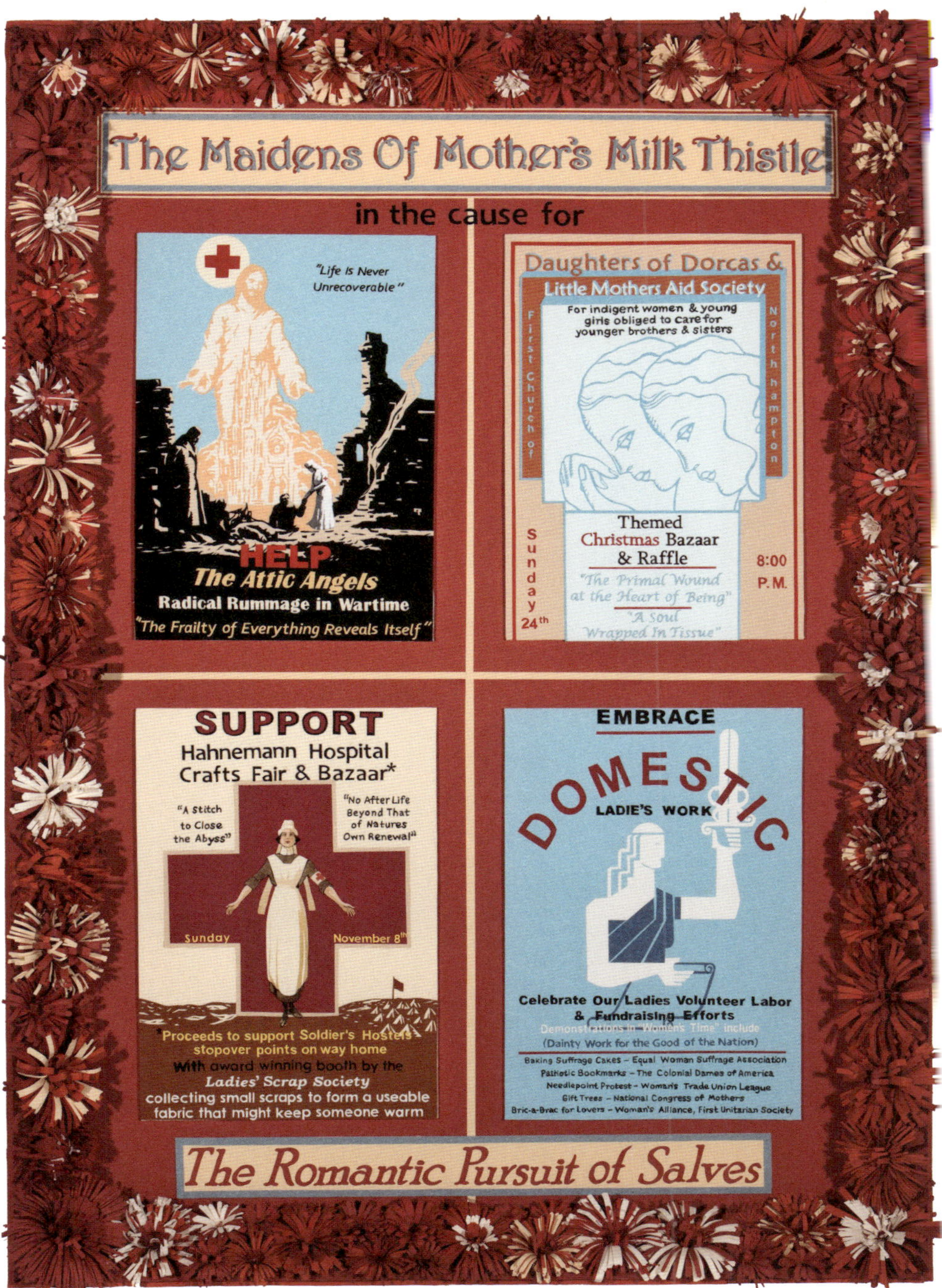

The Maidens Of Mother's Milk Thistle
in the cause for

"Life Is Never Unrecoverable"
HELP
The Attic Angels
Radical Rummage in Wartime
"The Frailty of Everything Reveals Itself"

Daughters of Dorcas &
Little Mothers Aid Society
First Church of
Northhampton
For indigent women & young girls obliged to care for younger brothers & sisters
Themed Christmas Bazaar & Raffle
Sunday 24th
8:00 P.M.
"The Primal Wound at the Heart of Being"
"A Soul Wrapped In Tissue"

SUPPORT
Hahnemann Hospital Crafts Fair & Bazaar*
"A Stitch to Close the Abyss"
"No After Life Beyond That of Natures Own Renewal"
Sunday
November 8th
*Proceeds to support Soldier's Hostels stopover points on way home
With award winning booth by the
Ladies' Scrap Society
collecting small scraps to form a useable fabric that might keep someone warm

EMBRACE
DOMESTIC
LADIE'S WORK
Celebrate Our Ladies Volunteer Labor & Fundraising Efforts
Demonstrations in "Women's Time" include
(Dainty Work for the Good of the Nation)
Baking Suffrage Cakes – Equal Woman Suffrage Association
Patriotic Bookmarks – The Colonial Dames of America
Needlepoint Protest – Woman's Trade Union League
Gift Trees – National Congress of Mothers
Bric-a-Brac for Lovers – Woman's Alliance, First Unitarian Society

The Romantic Pursuit of Salves

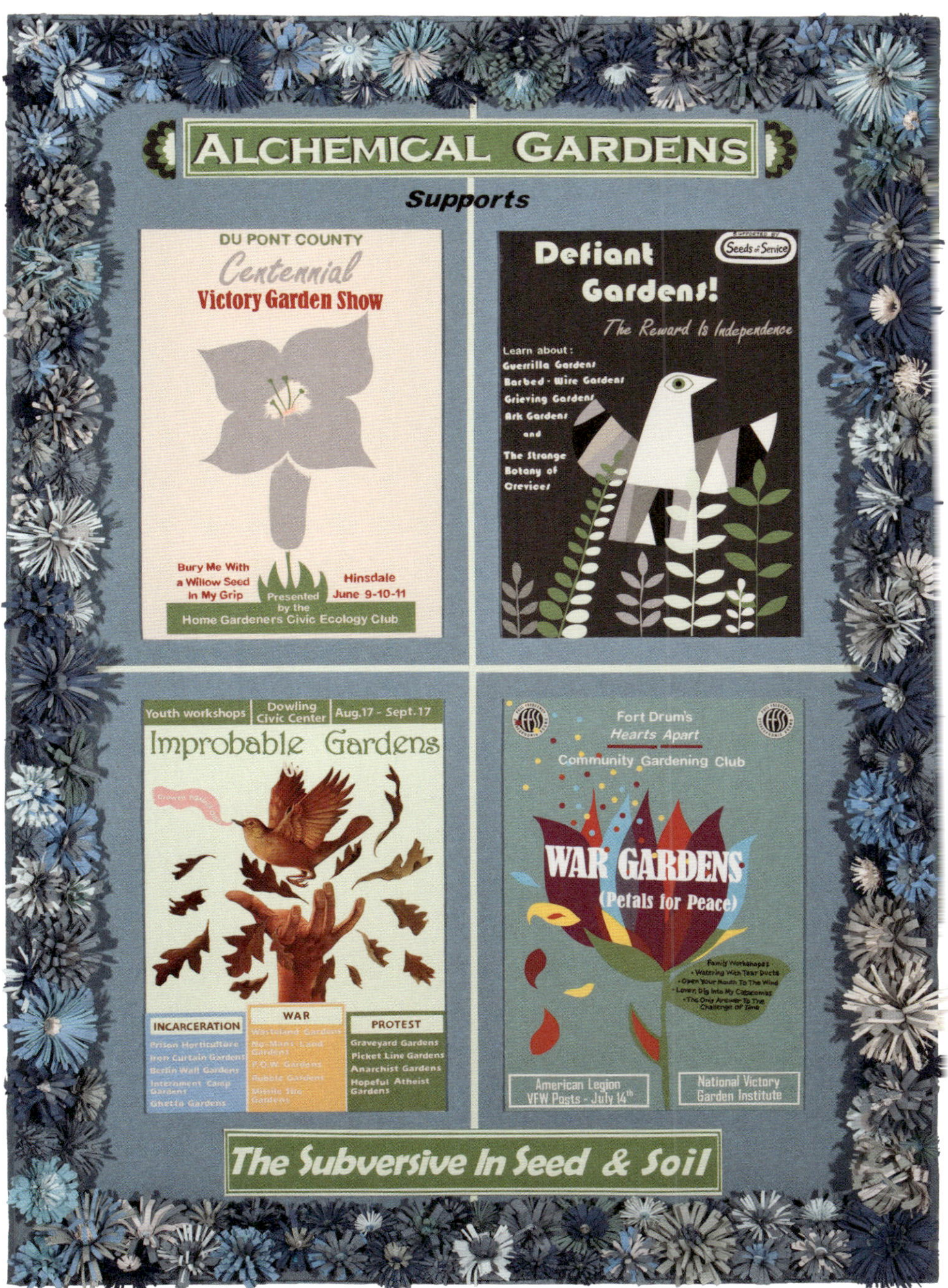
ALCHEMICAL GARDENS
Supports

DU PONT COUNTY
Centennial
Victory Garden Show
Bury Me With
a Willow Seed
In My Grip
Presented
by the
Home Gardeners Civic Ecology Club
Hinsdale
June 9-10-11

SUPPORTED BY
Seeds of Service
Defiant
Gardens!
The Reward Is Independence
Learn about:
Guerrilla Gardens
Barbed - Wire Gardens
Grieving Gardens
Ark Gardens
and
The Strange
Botany of
Crevices

Youth workshops
Dowling
Civic Center
Aug.17 - Sept.17
Improbable Gardens
INCARCERATION
Prison Horticulture
Iron Curtain Gardens
Berlin Wall Gardens
Internment Camp
Gardens
Ghetto Gardens
WAR
Wasteland Gardens
No-Mans-Land
Gardens
P.O.W. Gardens
Rubble Gardens
Missile Silo
Gardens
PROTEST
Graveyard Gardens
Picket Line Gardens
Anarchist Gardens
Hopeful Atheist
Gardens

Fort Drum's
Hearts Apart
Community Gardening Club
WAR GARDENS
(Petals for Peace)
Family Workshops
• Watering With Tear Ducts
• Open Your Mouth To The Wind
• Learn Dig Into My Catacombs
• The Only Answer To The
Challenge Of Time
American Legion
VFW Posts - July 14th
National Victory
Garden Institute

The Subversive In Seed & Soil

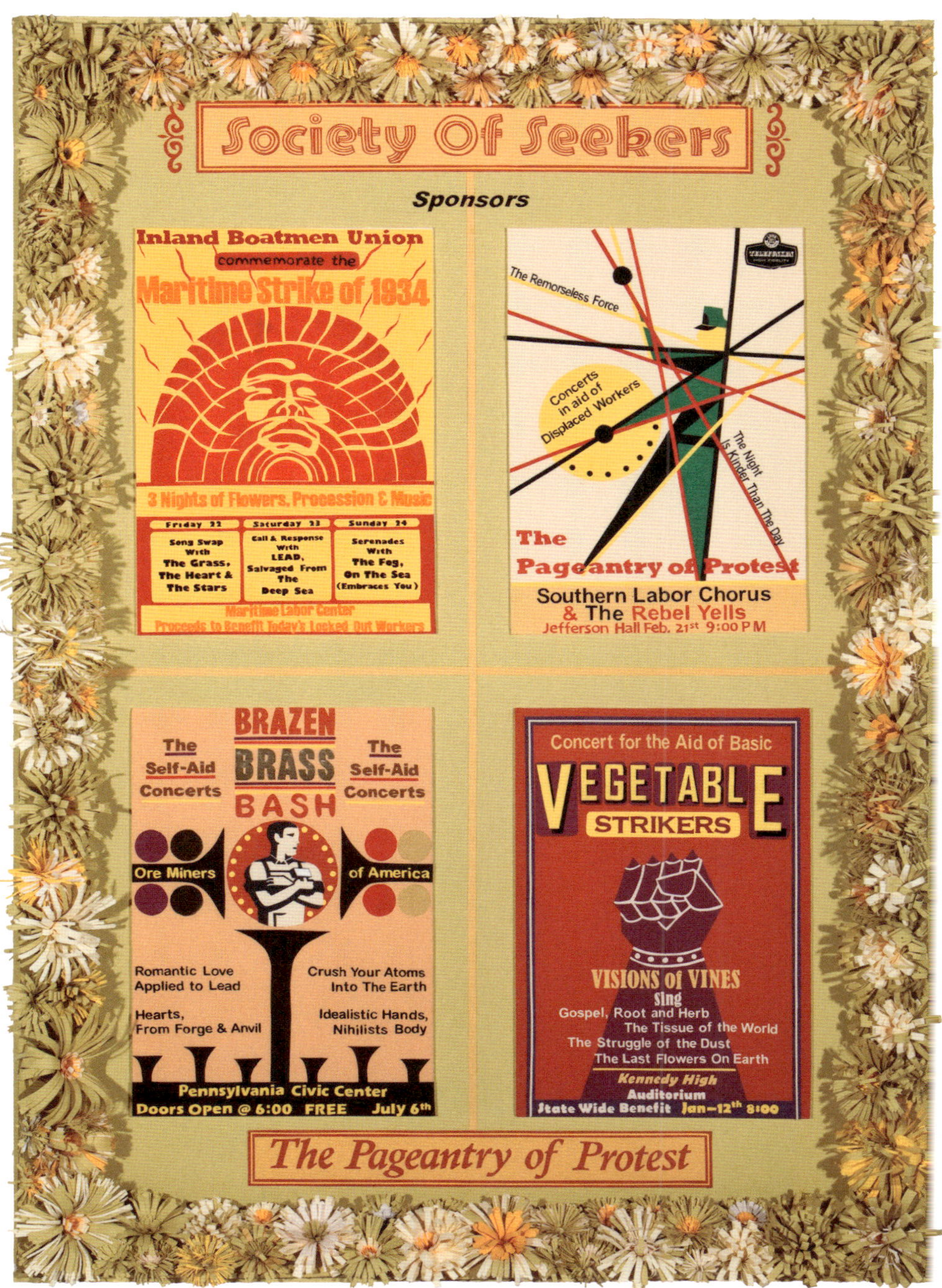

Society Of Seekers
Sponsors
Inland Boatmen Union
commemorate the
Maritime Strike of 1934
3 Nights of Flowers, Procession & Music
Friday 22
Song Swap
With
The Grass,
The Heart &
The Stars
Saturday 23
Call & Response
With
LEAD,
Salvaged From
The
Deep Sea
Sunday 24
Serenades
With
The Fog,
On The Sea
(Embraces You)
Maritime Labor Center
Proceeds to Benefit Today's Locked Out Workers
The Remorseless Force
Concerts
in aid of
Displaced Workers
The Night Is Kinder Than The Day
The
Pageantry of Protest
Southern Labor Chorus
& The Rebel Yells
Jefferson Hall Feb. 21st 9:00 PM
The
Self-Aid
Concerts
BRAZEN
BRASS
BASH
The
Self-Aid
Concerts
Ore Miners
of America
Romantic Love
Applied to Lead
Crush Your Atoms
Into The Earth
Hearts,
From Forge & Anvil
Idealistic Hands,
Nihilists Body
Pennsylvania Civic Center
Doors Open @ 6:00   FREE   July 6th
Concert for the Aid of Basic
VEGETABLE
STRIKERS
VISIONS of VINES
sing
Gospel, Root and Herb
The Tissue of the World
The Struggle of the Dust
The Last Flowers On Earth
Kennedy High
Auditorium
State Wide Benefit Jan—12th 8:00
The Pageantry of Protest

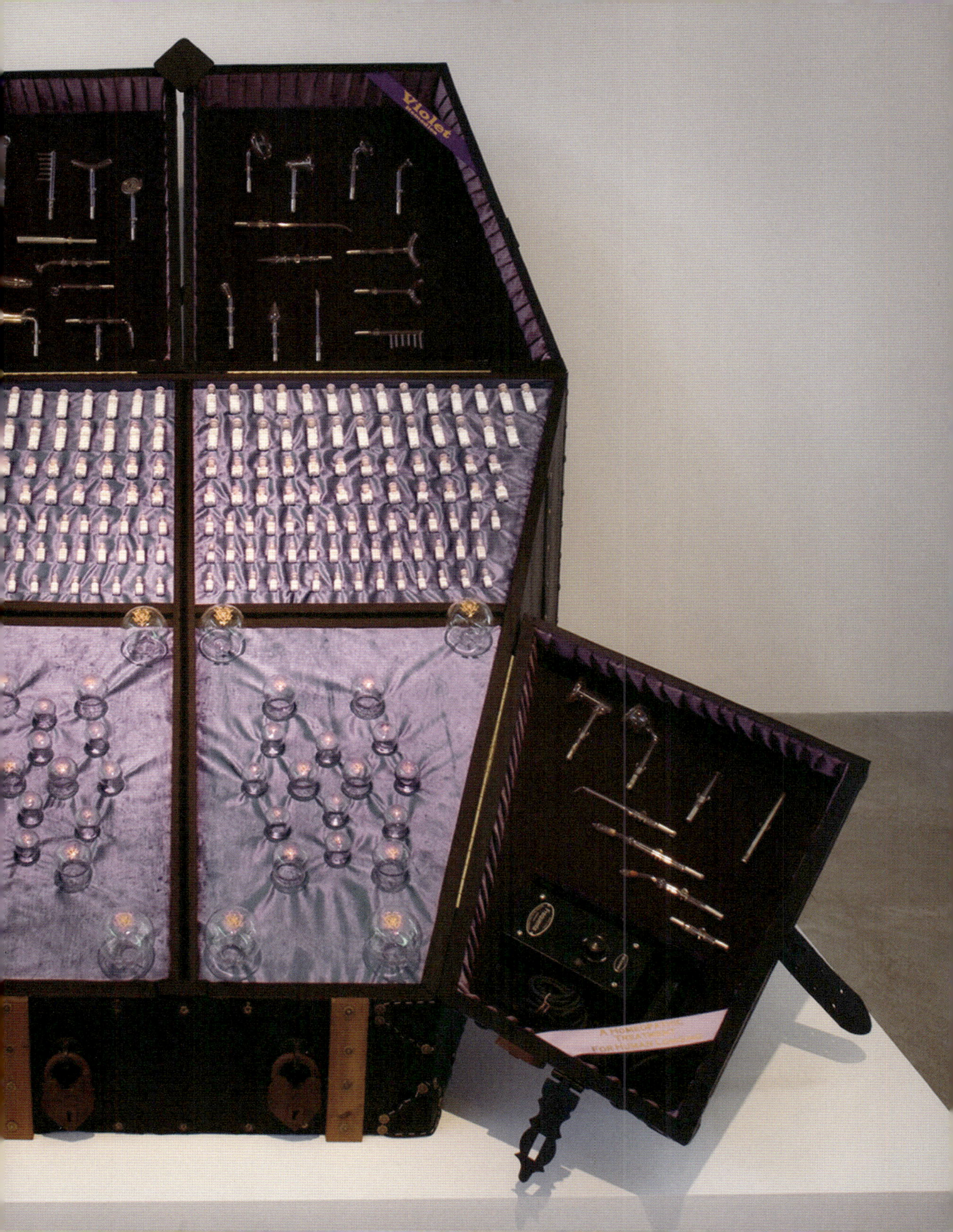
Violet
A HOMEOPATHIC
TREATMENT
FOR HUMAN AILMENTS

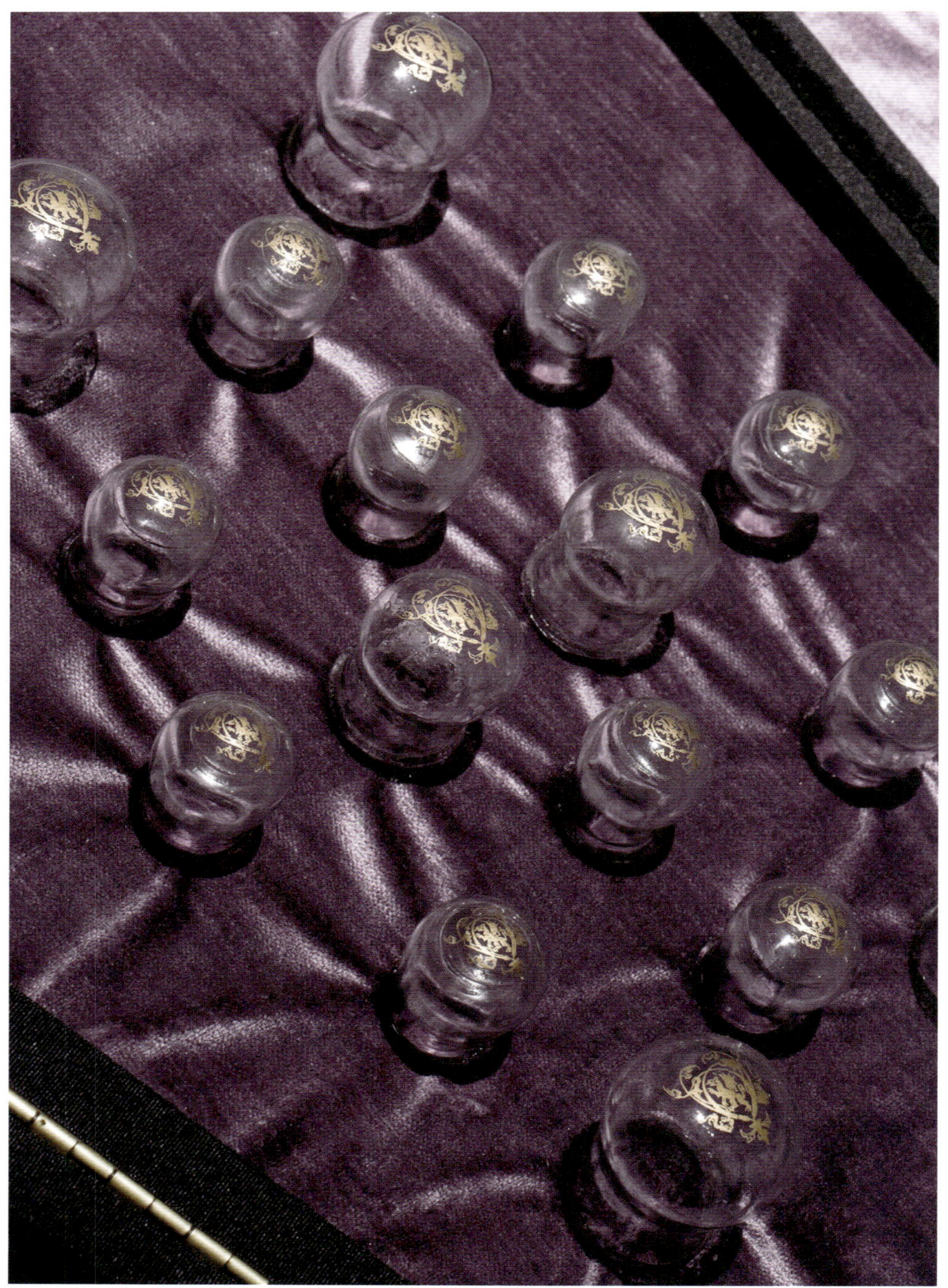

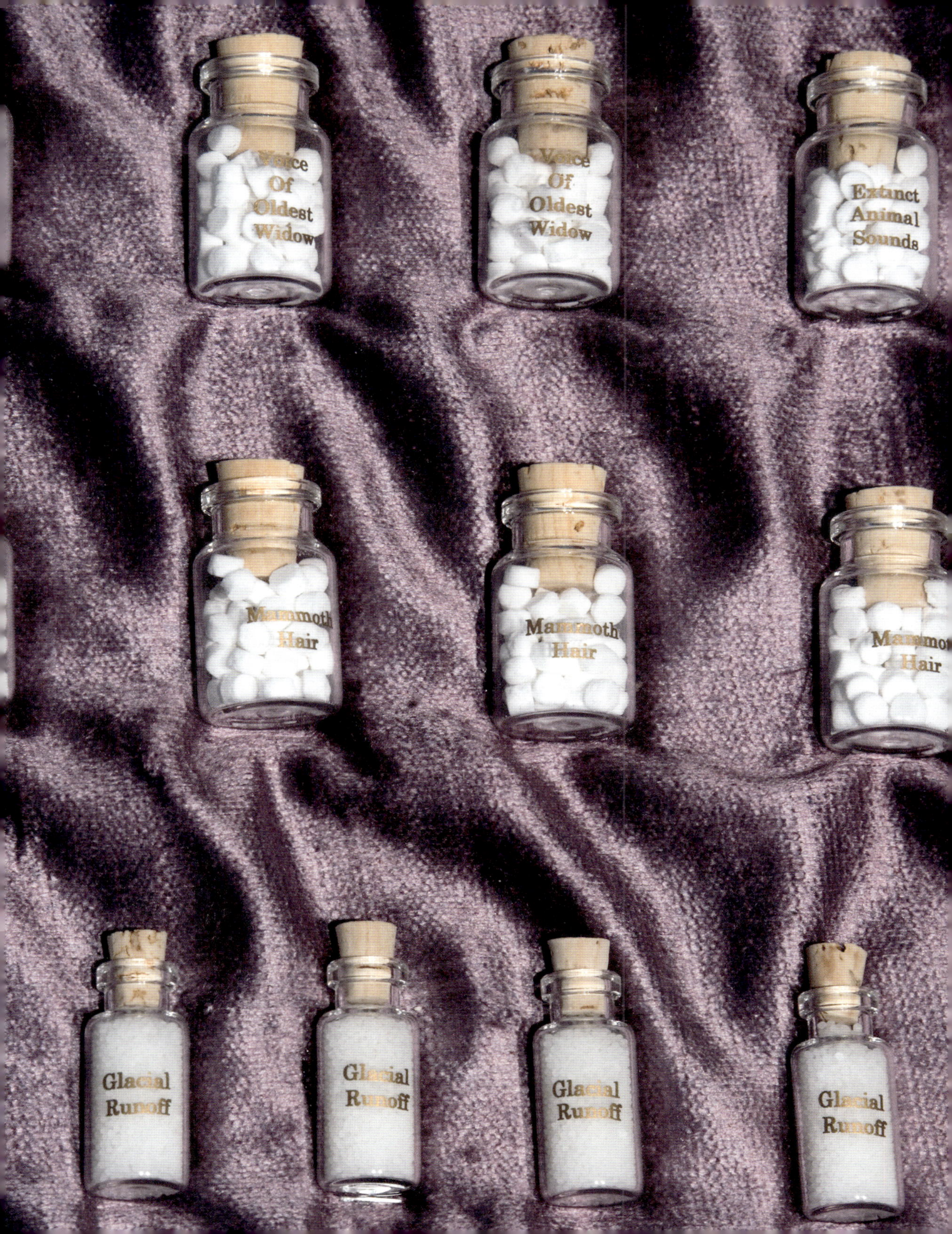

Voice
Of
Oldest
Widow
Voice
Of
Oldest
Widow
Extinct
Animal
Sounds
Mammoth
Hair
Mammoth
Hair
Mammoth
Hair
Glacial
Runoff
Glacial
Runoff
Glacial
Runoff
Glacial
Runoff

A HOMEOPATHIC TREATMENT FOR HUMAN LONGING 2008

Glass vials, vintage glass electrode wands, 19th-century
bloodletting cupping glass, various artist-made homeopathic
remedies (sound of glaciers melting, voice of oldest to ever live,
last heartbeats of loved one, million-year-old blossom,
million-year-old raindrop, deceased lovers' heartbeats, extinct animal
sounds, extinct languages), various custom-ordered remedies made
by professional homeopath (black amber, willow, tears, mammoth
hair, glacial runoff, voice of oldest widow, black swan bone dust,
Sylvia Plath's voice), velvet, silk, leather, ribbon,
brass, iron, cork, pine, typeset

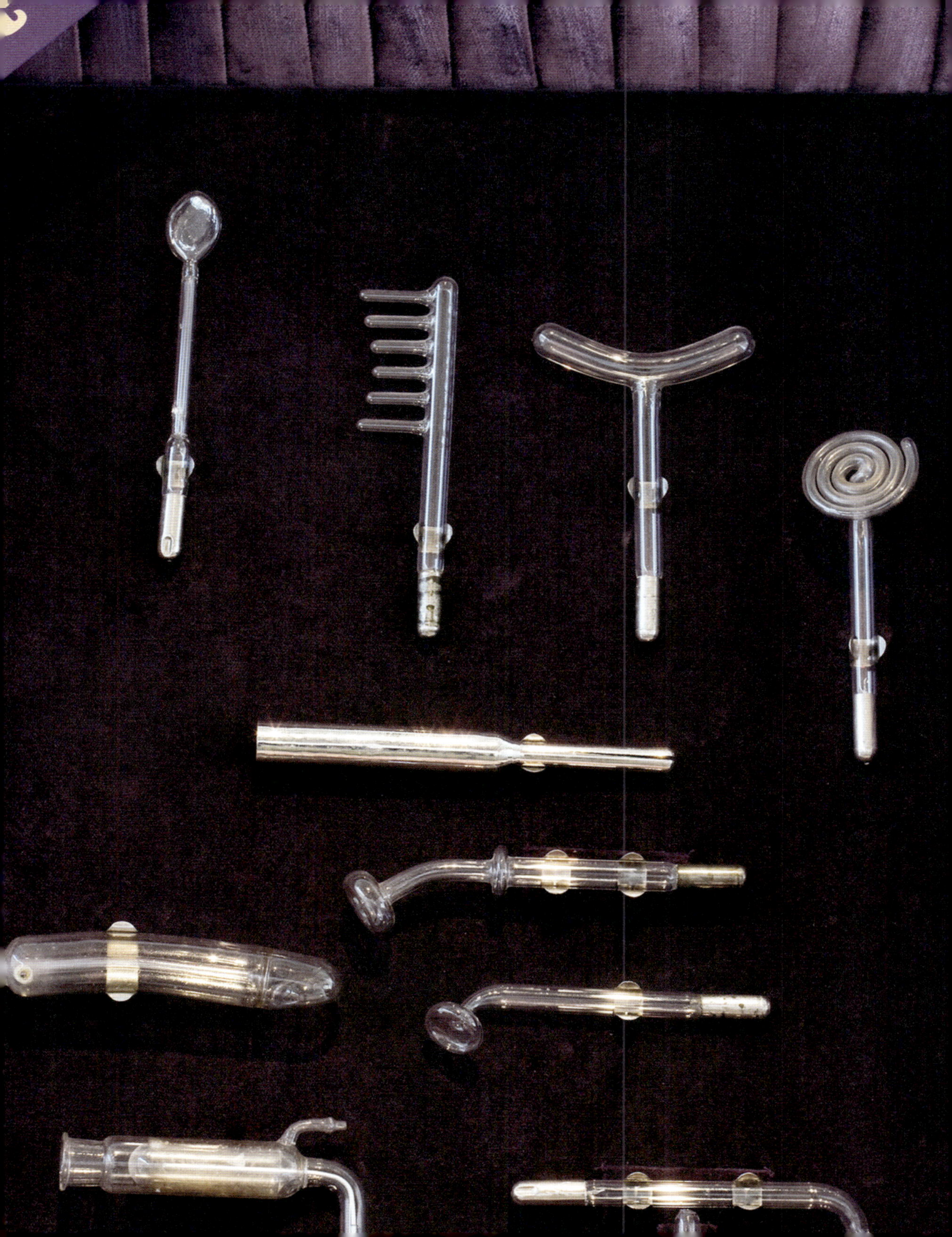

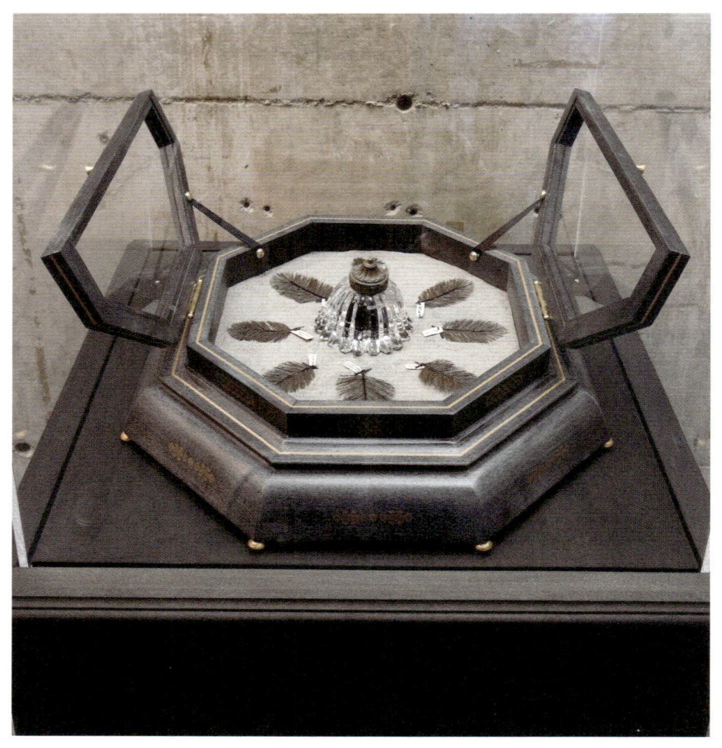

WORDS TREMBLE WITH THE THOUGHTS THEY EXPRESS 2008

Feathers made from stretched audiotape of the last recordings of

now-extinct birds and of now-extinct languages, glass inkwell,

homemade ink (lamp black, ground fulgurites [glass produced

by lightning strikes when heat from blast melts surrounding sand],

cuttlefish sepia), homemade paper, volcanic ash from

Mount St. Helens, ink dyed willow, brass, typeset

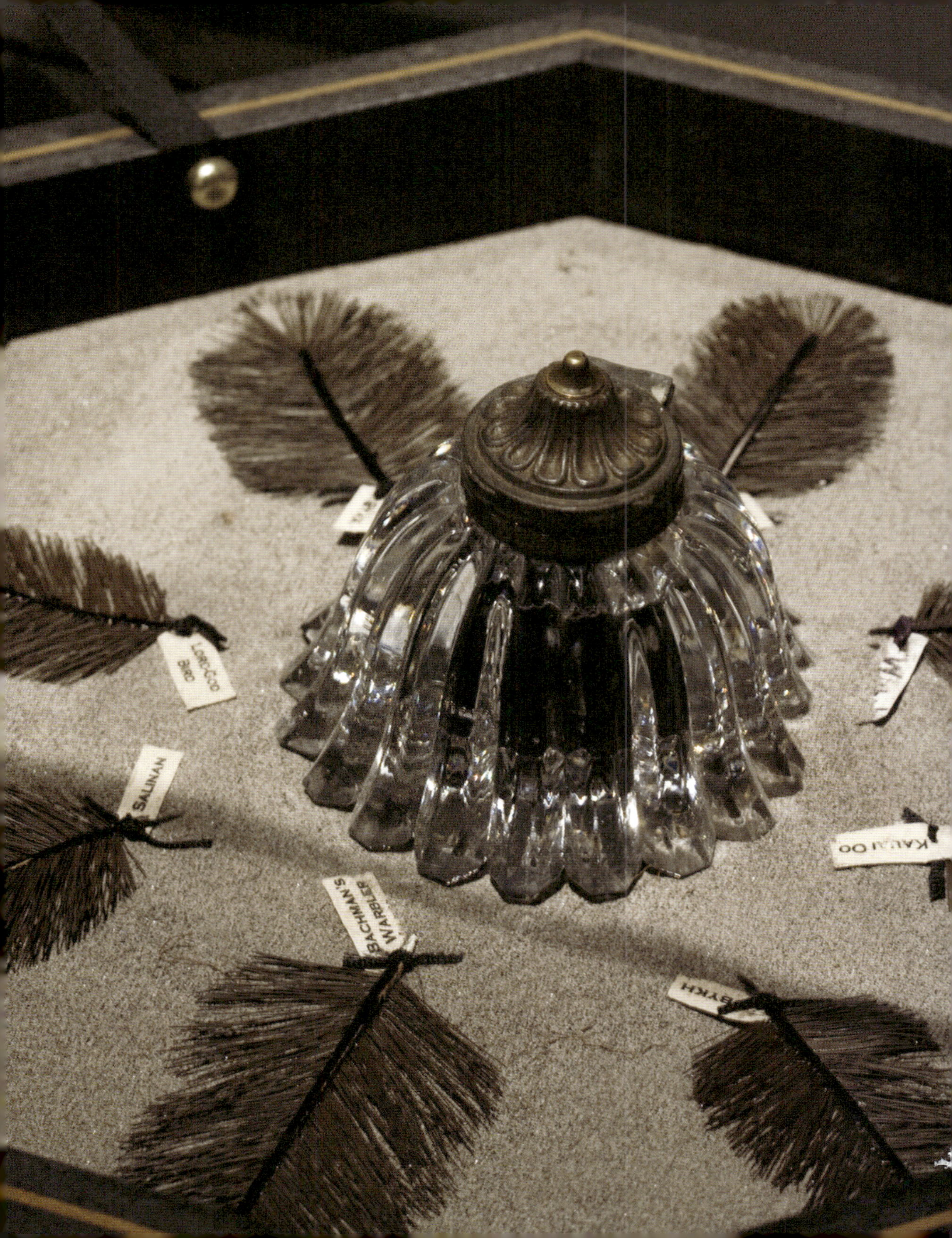

LONG-LEGGED BIRD
SALINAN
BACHMAN'S WARBLER
KAUAI OO

TALES OF THEODICIES 2010

Cut paper, cut album cover elements, colored pencil,

ribbon, foam core, glue

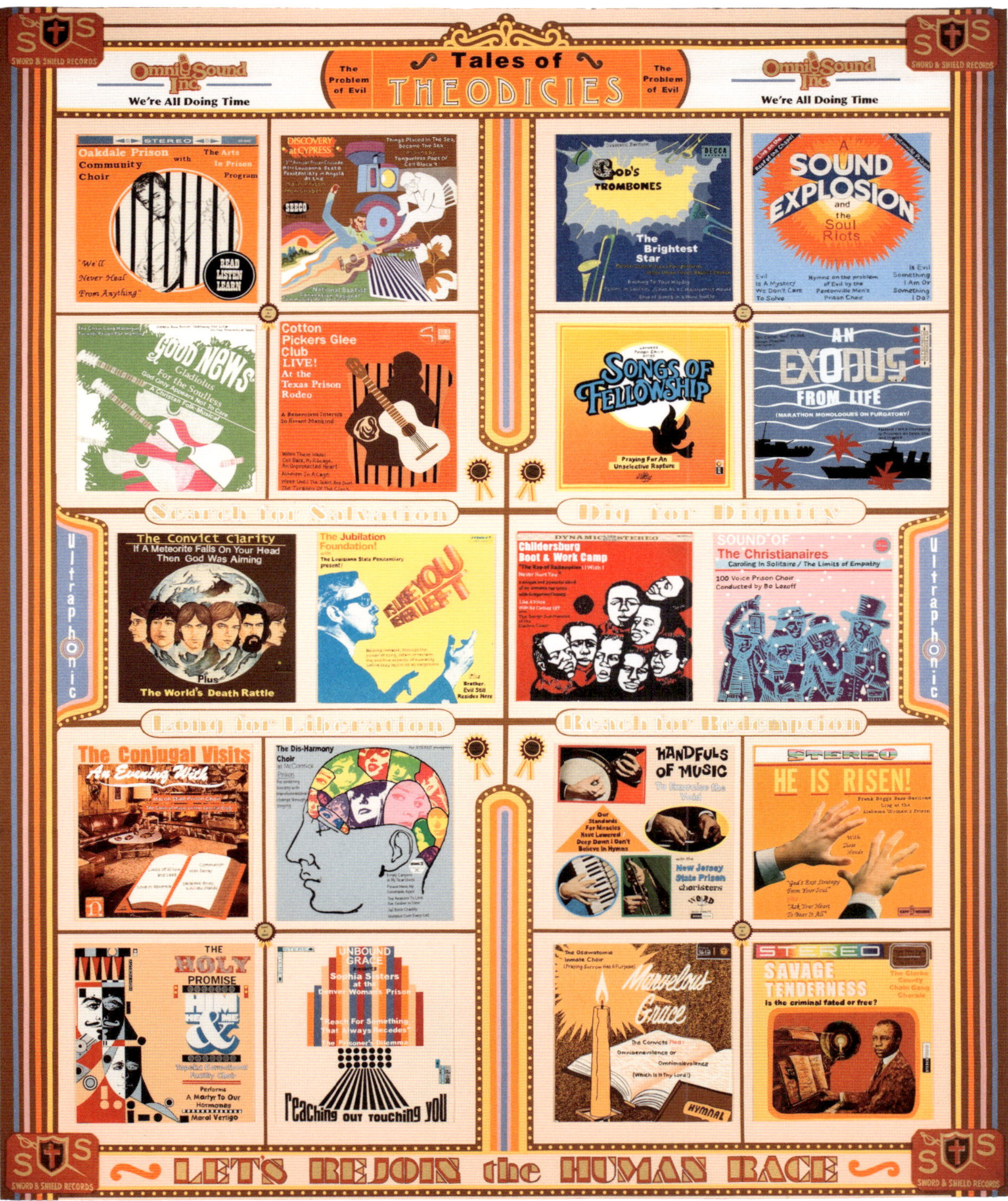

SWORD & SHIELD RECORDS
OmniSound Inc
We're All Doing Time
The Problem of Evil
Tales of THEODICIES
The Problem of Evil
OmniSound Inc
We're All Doing Time
SWORD & SHIELD RECORDS

STEREO
Oakdale Prison Community Choir
with
The Arts In Prison Program
"We'll Never Heal From Anything"
READ LISTEN LEARN

DISCOVERY at CYPRESS
SEECO
Things Placed In The Sea, Become The Sea
Tongueless Poet Of Cell Block 9

God's TROMBONES
DECCA
The Brightest Star

A SOUND EXPLOSION and the Soul Riots
Evil Is A Mystery We Don't Care To Solve
Hymns on the problem of Evil by the Pentonville Men's Prison Choir
Is Evil Something I Am Or Something I Do?

GOOD NEWS
Gladiolus For The Soulless
God Only Appears Not To Care
A Constant Folk Musical

Cotton Pickers Glee Club LIVE!
At the Texas Prison Rodeo
A Benevolent Interest In Errant Mankind

SONGS OF FELLOWSHIP
Praying For An Unselective Rapture

AN EXODUS FROM LIFE
(MARATHON MONOLOGUES ON PURGATORY)

Search for Salvation
Dig for Dignity
Ultraphonic
Ultraphonic

The Convict Clarity
If A Meteorite Falls On Your Head Then God Was Aiming
Plus
The World's Death Rattle

The Jubilation Foundation!
with
The Louisiana State Penitentiary Present!
HAVE YOU EVER LEFT
Old Brother, Evil Still Resides Here

DYNAMIC STEREO
Childersburg Boot & Work Camp
The Rap of Redemption / I Wish I Never Hurt You
Like A Voice With No Context Of
The Savage Subliminance of the Electric Chair

SOUND OF The Christianaires
Caroling In Solitaire / The Limits of Empathy
100 Voice Prison Choir
Conducted by Bo Lozoff

Long for Liberation
Reach for Redemption

The Conjugal Visits
An Evening With

The Dis-Harmony Choir
at McCormick Prison
STEREO

HANDFULS OF MUSIC
To Exercise the World!
Our Standards For Miracles Have Lowered
Deep Down I Don't Believe In Hymns
with the New Jersey State Prison Choristers
SWORD

STEREO
HE IS RISEN!
Frank Briggs Baritone Sing at the Alabama Women's Prison
With Jazz Hands
"God's Exit Strategy From Your Soul"
"Ask Your Heart To Bear It All"

THE HOLY PROMISE
HIM &
Performs
A Martyr To Our Hormones
Moral Vertigo

UNBOUND GRACE
presents
Sophia Sisters at the Denver Woman's Prison
Reach For Something That Always Recedes
The Prisoner's Dilemma
reaching out touching you

The Osawatomie Inmate Choir
(Praying Sorrow Has A Purpose)
Marvelous Grace
The Convicts Plead:
Omnibenevolence or Omnimalevolence
(Which Is It Thy Lord?)
HYMNAL

STEREO
SAVAGE TENDERNESS
Is the criminal fated or free?
The Clarke County Chain Gang Chorale

LET'S REJOIN the HUMAN RACE
SWORD & SHIELD RECORDS

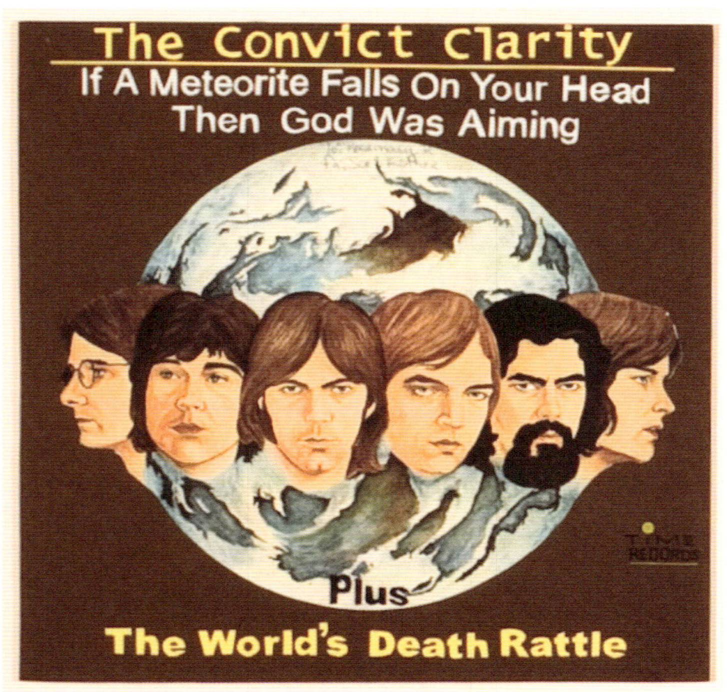

The Convict Clarity
If A Meteorite Falls On Your Head
Then God Was Aiming
Plus
The World's Death Rattle

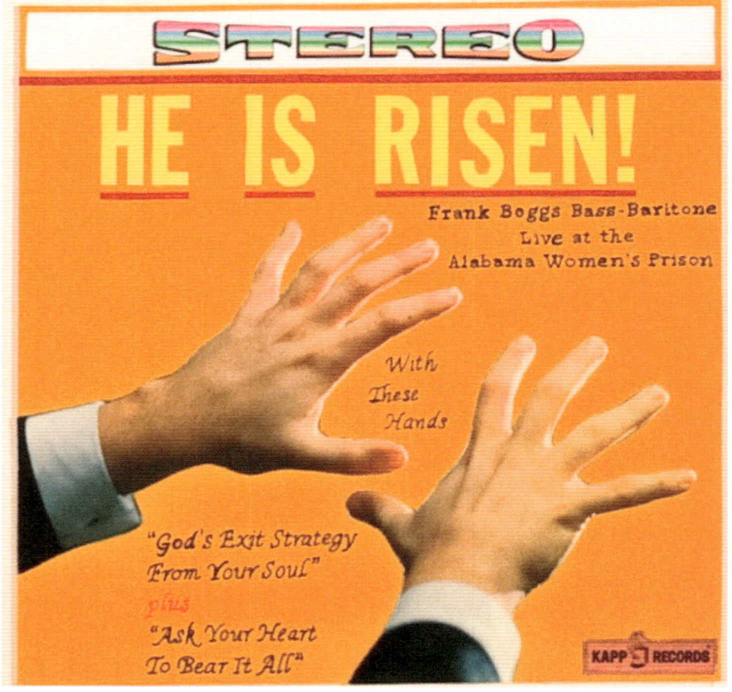

STEREO
HE IS RISEN!
Frank Boggs Bass-Baritone
Live at the
Alabama Women's Prison
With
These
Hands
"God's Exit Strategy
From Your Soul"
plus
"Ask Your Heart
To Bear It All"
KAPP RECORDS

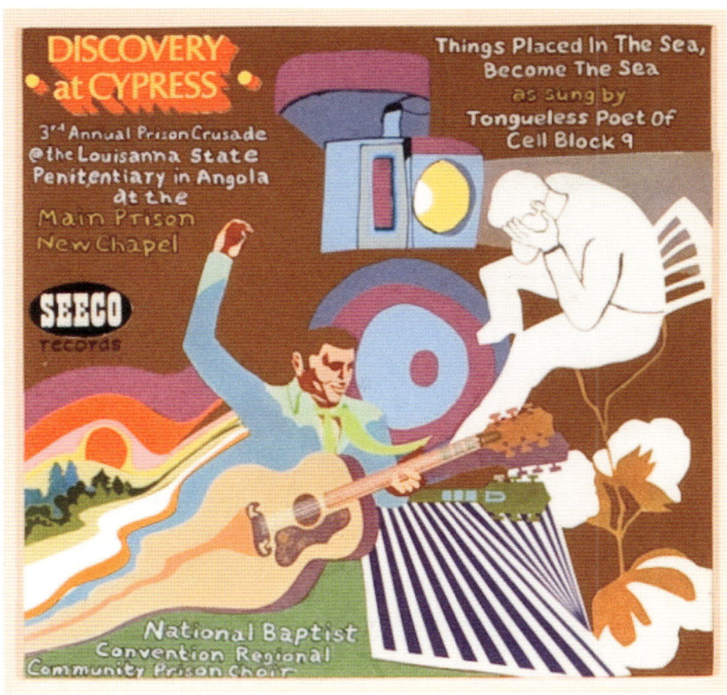
DISCOVERY at CYPRESS
3rd Annual Prison Crusade @ the Louisanna State Penitentiary in Angola at the Main Prison New Chapel
SEECO records
Things Placed In The Sea, Become The Sea
as sung by Tongueless Poet Of Cell Block 9
National Baptist Convention Regional Community Prison Choir

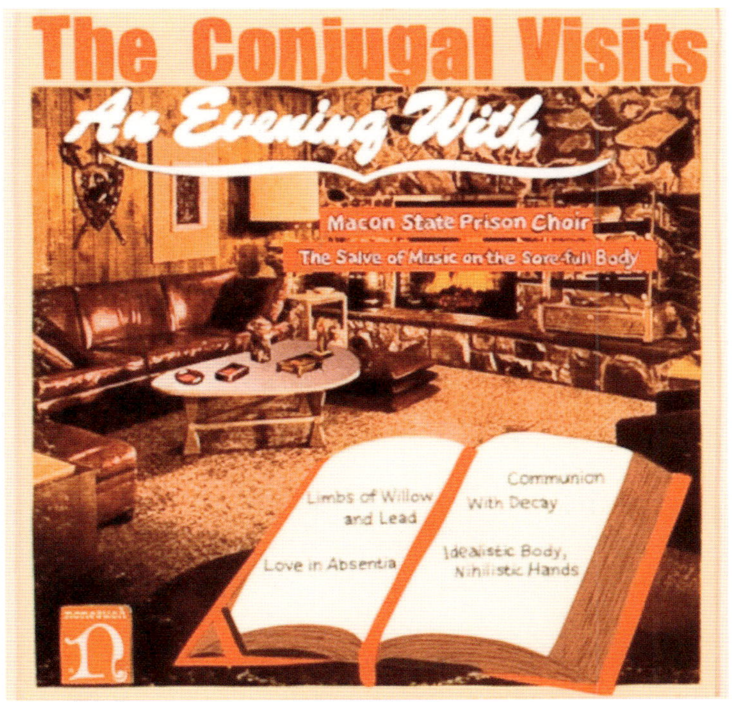
The Conjugal Visits
An Evening With
Macon State Prison Choir
The Salve of Music on the Sore-full Body
Limbs of Willow and Lead
Communion With Decay
Love in Absentia
Idealistic Body, Nihilistic Hands

THE COMMON DENOMINATOR OF EXISTENCE IS LOSS 2008

50,000-year-old extinct cave bear paws, human hand bones,

stretched and pulled audiotape of the earliest audio recording

of time (experimental clock, 1878), 19th-century mourning

ribbon, bocote, shellac, glass

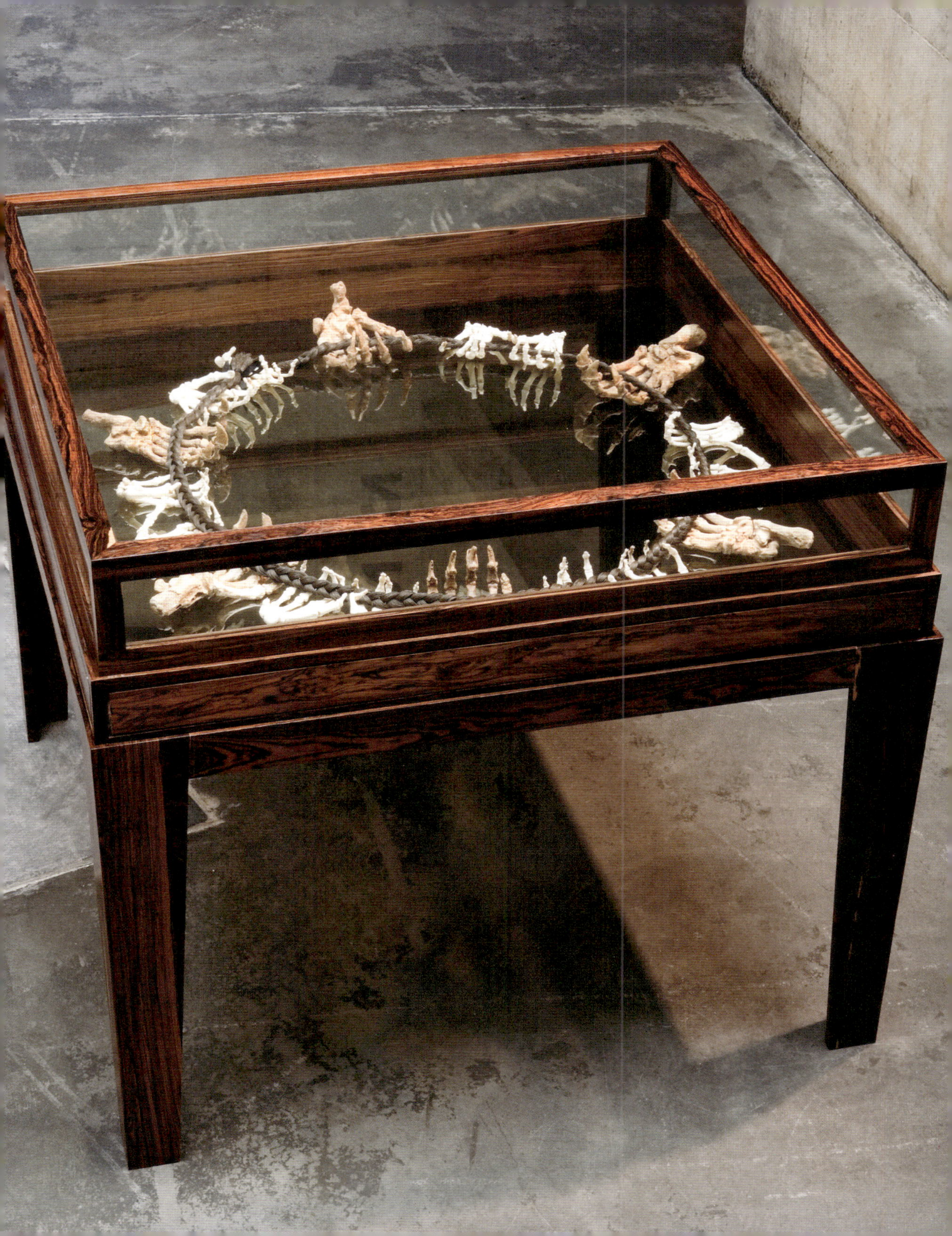

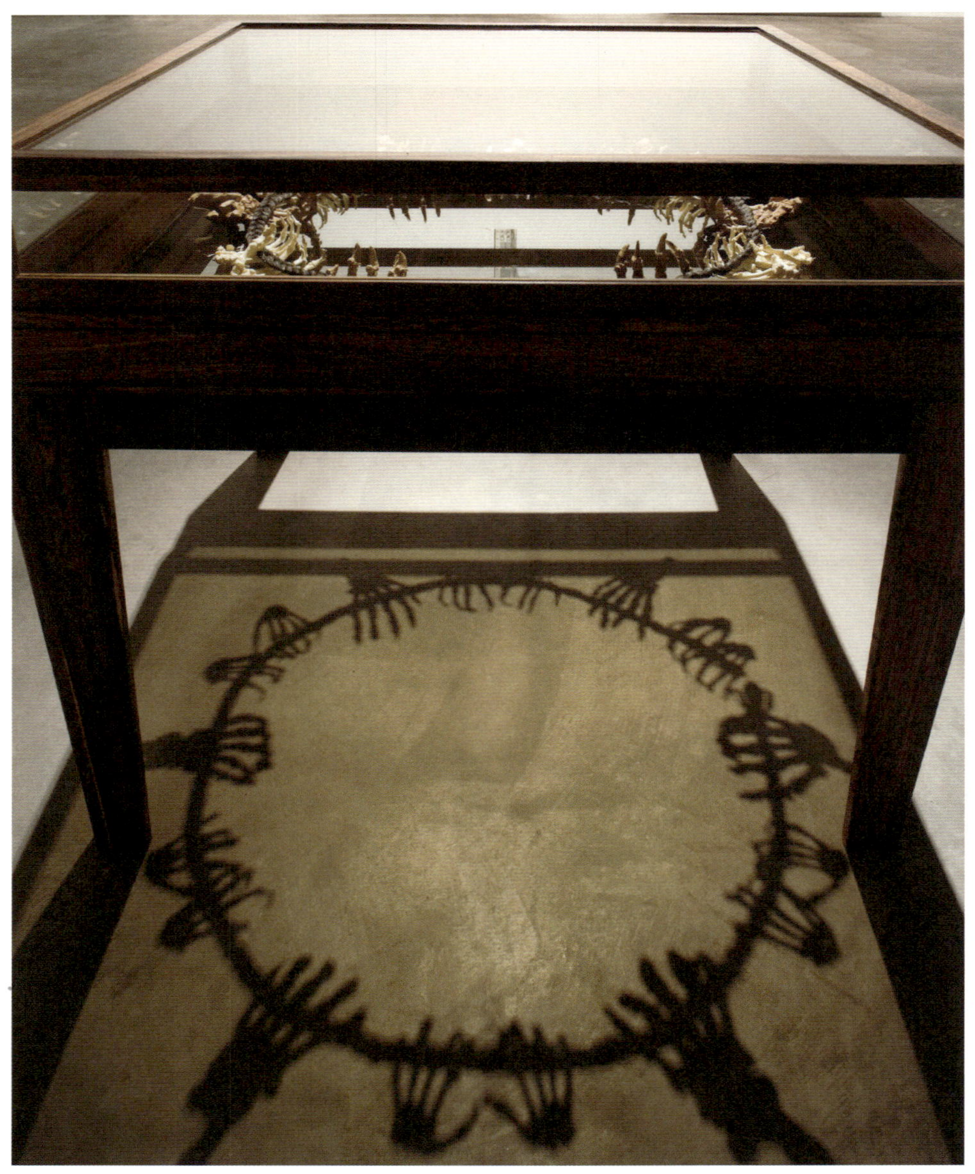

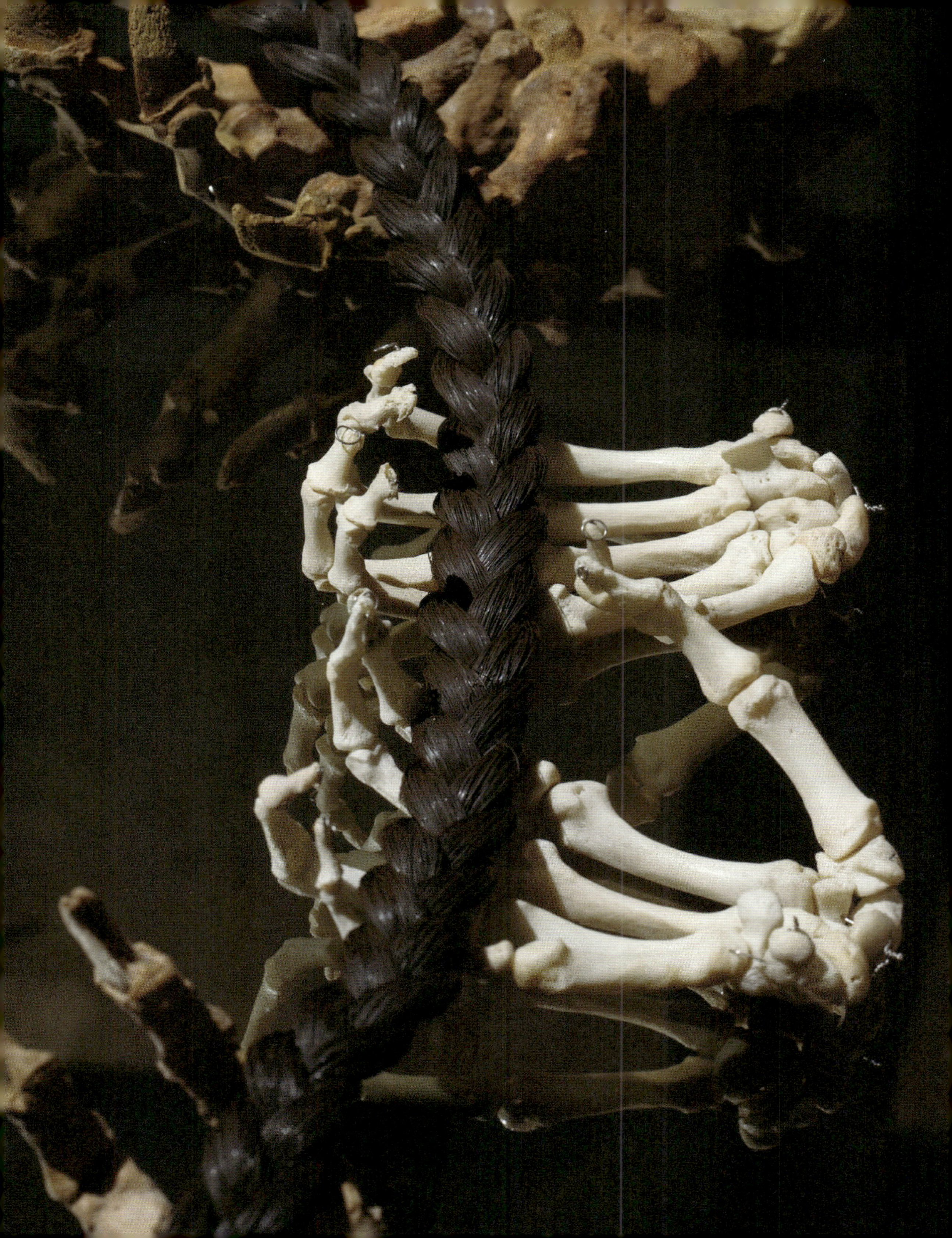

CANDLES UN-BURN, SUNS UN-SHINE, DEATH UN-DIES 2011

Inkjet print on custom vinyl wall paper, 61° curved wall

A collection of stage lights taken from the

album covers of live performances of now-deceased musicians

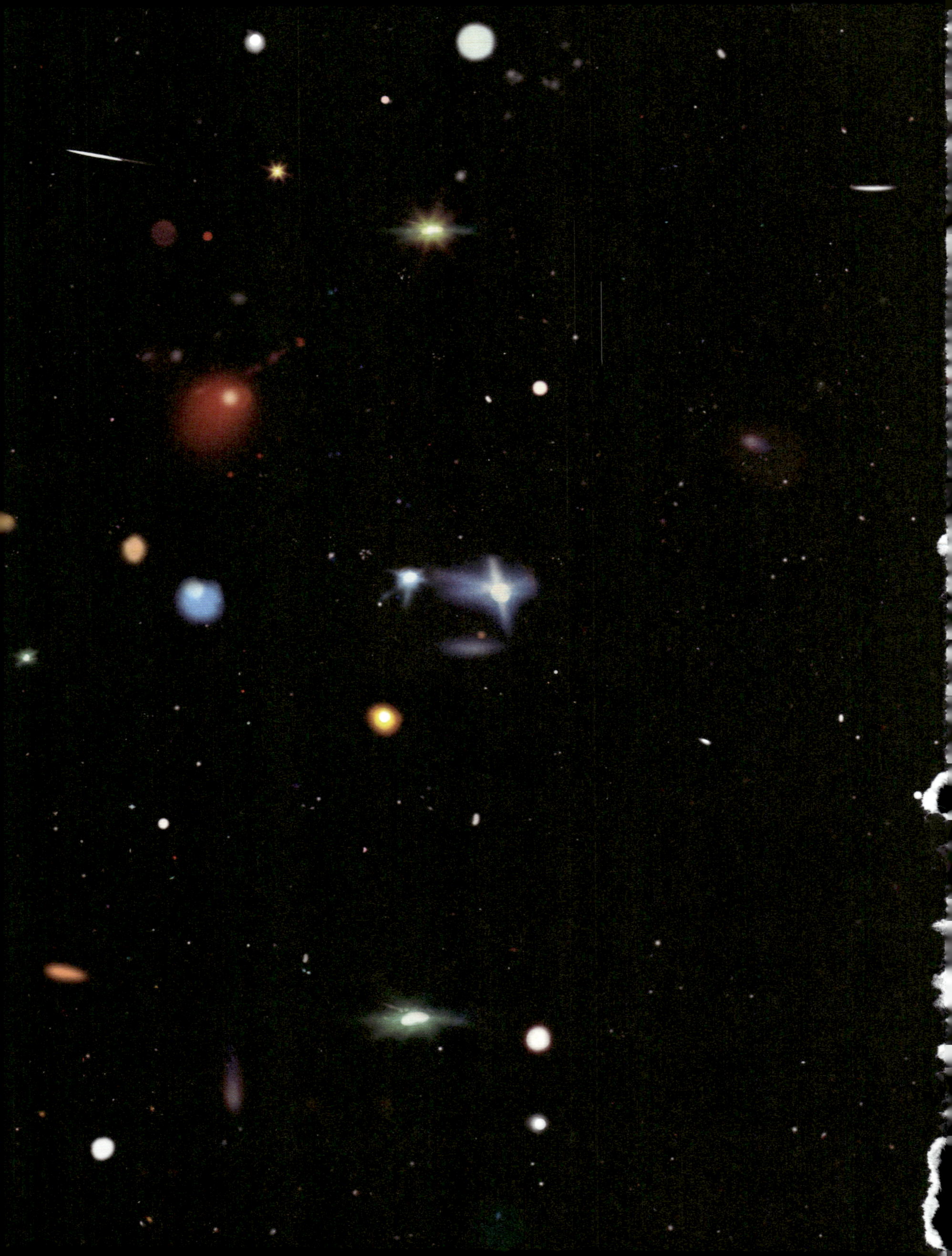

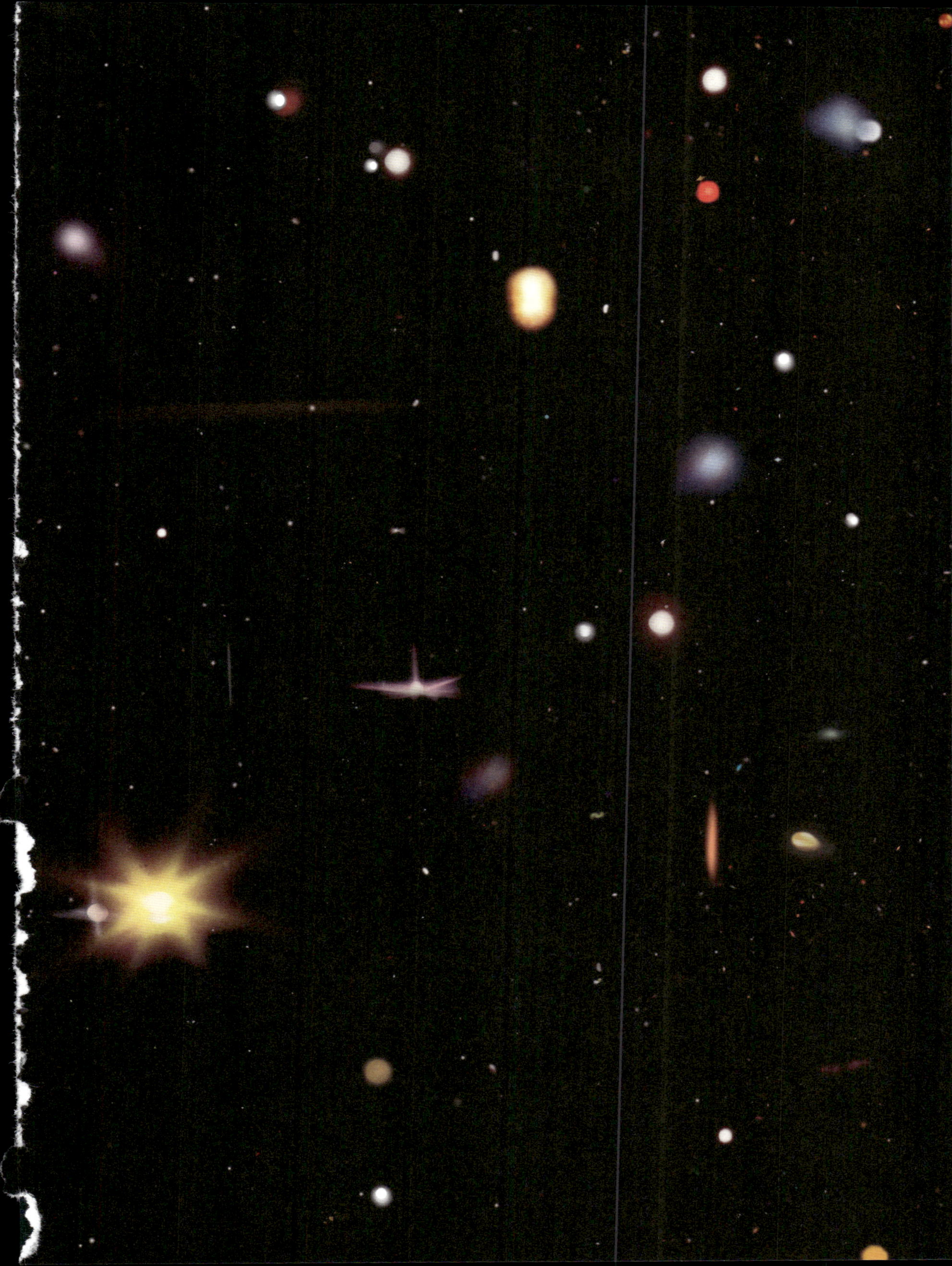

COLTRANE 1961/1962 CASH 1969

PETERSON 1980 VAUGHN 1959/1973

HENDRIX 1967/1969/1970

PAVAROTTI 1978 GAYE 1976

BOLAN 1974 HORNE 1969 GETZ 1964

CALLOWAY 1967 HOOKER 1978 NELSON 1969

HOPKINS 1964 BROWN 1969/1970

COOKE 1964 SHANNON 1972 GILLESPIE 1968

MONK 1963 LENNON 1972 PIAF 1955

REDDING 1966 ELLINGTON 1968

HOLIDAY 1956 MORRISON 1968 JACKSON 1961

SUN RA 1973 JONES 1967 SINATRA 1974

MANN 1966 SLIM 1973 MCRAE 1981

SEEING CLIMATE CHANGE

Naomi Oreskes

PROFESSOR OF HISTORY AND SCIENCE STUDIES AT THE UNIVERSITY OF
CALIFORNIA, SAN DIEGO / ADJUNCT PROFESSOR OF GEOSCIENCES AT THE
SCRIPPS INSTITUTION OF OCEANOGRAPHY

Why does climate change matter? Scientists speak to us of the changing chemistry of the atmosphere and its increasing concentration of greenhouse gases. They tell us of the impact these changes have on radiative transfer and the resulting increased heat reaching the Earth's surface in watts per meter squared. They tell us that some of the carbon dioxide produced by burning fossil fuels is being absorbed by the oceans, lowering the water's pH. And they tell us they have known all this for a long time.

This is all awfully abstract. Who has seen a watt per meter squared? Who has smelled the atmosphere's changing chemistry? Who has tasted radiative transfer? Who has felt the oceans' declining pH? The answer is no one—at least no human. None of us can see or feel or smell the rising carbon dioxide in our atmosphere. If greenhouse gases were purple and the sky were turning from blue to violet before our eyes, we might feel differently about climate change.

And this is the crux of the issue: how we *feel* about climate change. Most of us feel nothing. It's not that we are unfeeling people, it's just that we are busy with our daily lives. We get up and get dressed. We drive to work. We pick up the kids. We make dinner. We watch television. We pay the bills. We listen to music. If things are good and time and money permit, we enjoy a dinner out with friends, are captivated by a film, or relax on vacation. Climate change just isn't something that engages us on a daily basis. It isn't something we *experience*. It isn't an activity. While we get frustrated over traffic, kvell over our children, anticipate a vacation, or relax in the arms of a beloved, we just don't feel climate change.

There are exceptions. In the United States, in particular, some of us feel angry—angry at the implication that there is something wrong with our great society and the way we live. Angry at the implication that this is our fault. And in our anger we have turned to denial. We actively reject the scientific evidence, insisting that the climate has always varied, that what we are seeing might be caused by volcanoes or the sun, and that if the climate changes significantly in the future we can always adapt.

Even among those of us who more or less accept that the science is true, we are anxious about what it means for our futures. So if we are not angry, not in denial, we nevertheless push aside thinking about what we are doing to the world around us, the world that sustains us, the world upon which our lives, our societies, and our cultures depend. Denial is a powerful emotion, and it helps to suppress more disturbing feelings, like anxiety and fear. The denial of climate change is the denial of the anxiety and fear we would experience should we actively and consciously come to grips with what climate change is really all about.

And what is climate change really all about? In a word: loss. Climate change matters because of what we stand to lose.

Yet almost no one is talking about *that*. Almost no one is addressing the anticipation of loss that we should feel when we contemplate the radical changes we are unleashing on the planet that sustains us. No one, that is, except Dario Robleto. In his work, Robleto engages us in a remarkable conversation about evanescence, longing, and loss.

For the past 150 years, those of us living in the wealthy nations of the world—in North America, Europe, Australia, New Zealand, and Japan—have been living off stored wealth. The energy in fossil fuels was stored over millions of years of geological time, and we have been tapping it like money in the bank, an enormous planetary trust fund. Just like a trust fund, we didn't put it there; we simply inherited it. It's as if we were wanderers who settled in a new place only to find that the stores had been stocked for us, the root vegetables laid in, the wine aged and ready for us to drink. We were travelers who arrived at a hotel to find that the previous occupants had left a wardrobe of fine clothes and a pantry full of food. Energy in fossil fuels was a bottle of champagne waiting to be uncorked—and not just a bottle, but a whole wine cellar. Put this way, we realize that we have been incredibly, amazingly lucky.

We celebrated that good luck by having a party. We uncorked the champagne and put the trust fund to work. To our credit, we mostly made good use of it. We generated prosperity which, unlike in days of old, did not just flow to kings and pharaohs, but was shared by a large proportion of the population. We built beautiful cathedrals and interesting cities. We cultivated the arts and sciences, creating theater and painting, music and dance, physics and chemistry, medicine and dentistry. We invented materials not found in nature. We found cures for the afflictions that plagued our past. We built transportation networks that exceeded the imaginings of our most creative seers, so that an ordinary person could 'round the world not just in 80 days, but in 80 hours. We have sent men to the moon and brought them safely back. We've gone 20,000 leagues under the sea.

And as Robleto reminds us, we invented rock and roll.

And like those rockers—whom so many of us as teenagers longed to be—we got high on our success. We felt ourselves to be stronger, wiser, sexier, and more courageous than we really were. And like a stoned rocker, we did some foolish things. We convinced ourselves that we had created an economic system in which growth generated growth—economic activity generated economic activity. We talked of magic—the magic of the marketplace—and acted as if it were real. We imagined a world without limits. We thought we could fly.

When a few sages—modern-day Cassandras—warned us that matters might be otherwise, we didn't listen. We brushed them aside as foolish or cowardly. If they were men, we faulted them for lacking imagination. If they were women, we dismissed them as hysterical. The history of the western world since the industrial revolution and the rise of efficient, market-based economies was a good-news story, and we didn't want anyone to spoil it. We didn't want anyone to ruin the party. We didn't want anyone to say, "Yes, but…."

Now scientists have spoiled the fun. They have pointed out something that, in hindsight, might have been obvious in the first place: that when we do stuff, we create refuse. You can't have a party without clearing out the bottles in the morning. And it turns out you cannot tap the energy in fossil fuels without producing greenhouse gases that make the atmosphere hotter and the oceans more acidic. So we have a problem. Fossil fuels have not run out; there is still plenty of money in the bank. And yet we find we cannot—dare not—spend it. No wonder we are upset.

Or, to return to the party analogy, it's as if there were still plenty of alcohol left, but our parents have returned home unexpectedly, yelled at us, and forbidden us to drink any more. Like teenagers, we are angry at our parents, blaming them, rejecting them, determined to rebel against their authority. Scientists are our parents when it comes to global warming, and we have rejected their authority. Who are they to tell us what to do?

Is there a way out of the impasse? Yes, but perhaps not through more science. Perhaps through the opposite—or at least via a complement: by thinking less about the scientific facts and more about what they mean.

Scientific evidence tells us there isn't a planetary trash bin in which to throw our greenhouse-gas garbage. We *thought* the atmosphere and the oceans were the trash can, or at least we acted as if they were. We were wrong. The greenhouse gases didn't just vanish into space or dissolve into the deep ocean. They stayed where they were (more or less), where they changed the chemistry of the atmosphere and oceans and increased the heat that was warming the surface of the Earth.

What does this mean for us? It means we have to change the way we live. We either have to stop tapping the trust fund—and perhaps become a lot poorer—or find another source of wealth. We have to stop drawing on the trust fund and go out and get a job. In practical terms, this means developing energy sources that do not produce greenhouse gases. Those energy sources exist, but they tend to be expensive, so in the future we may have to spend more money to maintain the same quality of life. Either way, there's a good chance that we just won't be as rich as we are now, and that is a sobering thought.

The list of what we stand to lose is very great. Beyond our material standard of living, paid for by the fossil-fuel trust fund, many treasures are now at risk. They include whole nations at or close to sea level, such as Tuvalu and Maldives, and the languages and cultures that may be carried with them beneath the rising seas. They include historic monuments and cities at sea level, such as Venice and Key West. They include charismatic animals, like the iconic polar bear, whose habitat may vanish in a warmer world, as well as thousands of other species whose ranges may shrink beyond the point of no return. And they include the two greatest wonders of the natural world—coral reefs and tropical rain forests—both severely threatened and already showing signs of stress. We live in a world of astonishing natural beauty, a world that never ceases to amaze when one takes the time to live in it. Much of that world is now at risk.

And then there is the ultimate loss: death. Increasingly around the globe we are seeing troubling signs that extreme weather events are becoming more extreme. In summer 2010, Russia and neighboring countries saw the highest recorded temperatures in their history, with more than 500 wildfires killing at least 52 people, destroying 2,000 homes, and charring almost 700 square miles. Many people were sickened from carbon monoxide poisoning, and still more may suffer ill effects from radioactive debris left over from the 1986 nuclear accident in Chernobyl, Ukraine, remobilized by the flames. In

China, more than 700 people were killed and more than 1,000 were missing after flooding, which also destroyed 7 million hectares of farmland and 645,000 houses. In Pakistan, the worst floods in that nation's history affected nearly 14 million people—substantially more than the Indian Ocean tsunami and the Haitian earthquake combined. In Australia, as the books closed on a drought of historic proportions in a land that is already the driest inhabited continent on the planet, bushfires raged near Sydney in winter, long before the summer fire season began. This was followed by catastrophic flooding in Queensland—the costliest natural disaster in Australian history. In the United States, in spring 2011, the Army Corps of Engineers deliberately flooded millions of acres of productive farmland to save towns and cities as the Missouri and Mississippi rivers swelled to record proportions. Meanwhile, tornadoes ripped their way out of tornado alley and into Alabama, only to be followed by a "monster" tornado that shredded homes, cars, and hospitals in Joplin, Missouri, leaving a path of death and destruction that made a mockery of the best-laid emergency management plans.

Scientists have been loath to link any one of these events to climate change, because climate is by definition a pattern, and one event, no matter how awful, does not a pattern make. But they have also been reluctant to talk about the pattern, about the mounting toll of death and destruction, or even about loss more abstractly, because it violates their sense of rationality.

Science is about what we know—through charts and graphs, observation and experiment, data and measurement—rather than what we feel.

Paradoxically, the mounting scientific evidence has permitted many of us to remain in denial, because while the charts and graphs enable scientists to tell us that we know anthropogenic climate change is under way, they do not empower the experts to communicate what is at stake. Nor do they enable us to articulate what we feel about the issue or act upon those feelings. This is a problem because, with some exceptions, most of us do not act upon what we know. We act upon what we feel. When there is a battle between the heart and the head, the heart will generally win. As the poet Beth Kope has noted, the heart is no mere muscle inside the rib cage, it is the "small moon in our body that commands our tides."

In order to act on climate change, we need to take the full measure of its meaning. We need to list the losses, acknowledge the anxiety, feel the fear. We need to understand that if we don't do something, we shall in the future be living in an impoverished world—both literally and metaphorically.

A great deal is at stake. Time is running out. We no longer have access to the trust fund. And it is not just enough to know this in our heads. We need to feel it in our hearts. We need to let that small moon pull us toward acknowledgement, toward action.

The people who reject the scientific evidence are not being entirely irrational. In their hearts they realize what is at stake. They enjoy the life they live now, and they don't want to change it. They don't want to be poorer. They are right to be afraid of what we stand to lose. What they are wrong about is in thinking that if we ignore the problem, it will go away.

Dario Robleto's work goes straight to the heart of this issue because it makes us confront loss. His work makes us *feel* climate change. In the earlier exhibition, *Human/Nature: Artists Respond to a Changing Planet,* Robleto explored the complex terrain of grieving and loss, taking inspiration from two very different sources: scientists studying the shrinking glaciers in Waterton/Glacier International Peace Park, as well as Victorian mourning practices. When I first saw this exhibit, I found myself weeping copiously. I stood there helplessly, wondering, who *was* this person, whom I had never met and knew nothing of, yet whose work had commanded not just my attention, but my soul? Here was an artist who had found a path right into the center of the meaning of climate change.

The glaciers in Glacier National Park have persisted since the last ice age came to a close some 10,000 years ago. Today, those glaciers are rapidly melting, victims of global warming. In 1850 there were some 150 glaciers in the park. Today there are 26 and that number is expected to reduce to zero by 2020 if current climate warming rates remain the same. During his research in the park, Robleto was struck by the vast discrepancy in time between the millennia needed to make the glaciers and the miniscule amount of time needed by humans to alter them. As Robleto began studying this phenomenon in other parts of the world, he realized one of the great ironies and unforeseen consequences of the world's glaciers and tundra melting is that as they melt new fossils are coming to light, released from the ice in which they have been trapped for thousands of years. These fossils are a boon to paleontologists, providing valuable information about the past, and in some areas an actual new economic resource to villagers who sell the freshly released fossils to fossil hunters, yet they come at the price of the majestic glaciers and tundra that once held them. As these fossils come to life, they also remind us that many Pleistocene mammals were driven to extinction by human predation, just as numerous species are today threatened by human-driven climate change.

The multilayer quality of loss is reflected in Robleto's exploration of the complex mourning practices of our Victorian forebears, who went for many months and sometimes years after the loss of a loved one wearing complex patterns of clothing and ribbons with details signifying their relation to the deceased, and thus the approximate degree of their loss. The Victorians may have been sexually repressed, but they knew how to grieve, literally wearing their broken hearts on their sleeves.

The Victorians left us copious evidence of their grief in the remains of their material culture, evidence Robleto puts to use in startlingly creative ways: refashioning, re-envisaging, and re-creating diverse materials, and inviting us to reconsider their meanings, past and present. In doing so, he challenges us to consider why we, in contrast to the Victorians, seem to be singularly unable to mourn, to grieve, or even to discuss death. For, as Robleto notes, we are staggeringly mute in the face of life's most important reality: finitude. Intellectually, we know that climate change is the result of finitude—that our planet is not limitless, and that time, space, and resources are all bound, even if we do not comprehend those bounds. And when we come up against boundaries—up against limits, up against loss—we sit facing it, unable to discuss it, just as it has become perhaps the most important thing that demands our attention and discussion.

Perhaps that is no coincidence.

In the current exhibit, *Survival Does Not Lie In The Heavens*, Robleto returns to the themes of frailty, death, loss, and the multifarious ways in which we fight finitude, struggle for transcendence, and rage against the dying of the light.

In *The Boundary of Life Is Quietly Crossed*, he calls our attention to the ironic brevity of longevity. For some time, Robleto has been paying attention to supercentenarians—men and women who have lived for more than 110 years, defying odds and finding flexibility in what would appear to be the ultimate inflexible boundary. Robleto is fascinated by the outer edge of human existence and makes a practice of tracking supercentenarians, learning about them, monitoring them, researching them, and recording their voices. Then, in signature Robleto fashion, he manipulates those audiotapes, refashioning them into hair lockets and blending them with other materials that recapitulate and resonate with themes of life and death, knowledge and uncertainty, nature and artifice.

Robleto re-imagines the obituary notices of these remarkable humans, creating a plaque for each one with written testimonial to their lives. In doing so he celebrates their lives, their persistence, even while anticipating (and accepting the inevitability of) their ends. And as Robleto makes and adds new cases for new individuals as they enter the supercentenarian ranks, the exhibit lives and grows. The installation itself denies finitude.

It takes a long time to reach the position of supercentenarian, and then one stays only briefly. Perhaps there is a metaphor in this for the length of time it has taken human civilization to conquer nature, before nature conquered us.

In *The Ark of Frailty*, Robleto focuses on Lazarus species—plants and animals thought to be extinct yet discovered to be extant, at least marginally so. Once again, we sit on the edge of existence—exploring the boundary of life and death, of presence and absence—for in most cases, if these species are not actually extinct, their numbers are so low that they will be soon. Their resurrection, much like the time supercentenarians enjoy their special status, is fleeting.

One might take despair from the short duration of this resurrection, yet the message of this installation is joyful. It is a celebration of the persistence of life, even as it acknowledges the inevitability of death. For in discovering these persistent survivors, scientists, naturalists, bird-watchers, and Robleto himself feel a profound joy that death has not come, that what seemed final was just not quite, and that perhaps there is a chance for long-term survival. The light has not yet died. And so long as the ashes are warm, the fires may yet be rekindled. Robleto clearly clings to this hope, just as his celebration of supercentenarians reminds us that even as these people slip from life, their achievement in resisting death longer than the rest of us is something to be admired, acknowledged, recalled, and remembered. In both these works, we see a profound sense of acknowledgement—that these things, these people, these species have been here, have struggled for existence, and have remained for a bit longer than anyone expected. They fought back against oblivion. They fought back against the dying of the light. And in this is a message of hope, that there may yet be a chance for us to fight back and survive, too.

Survival, persistence, and resurrection are persistent themes for

Robleto, and in his work, survival often takes the form of resurrection, as he turns old objects into new materials and new materials into would-be old objects. Bones, rocks, paper, vinyl records, melted earth, and who knows what else find new form, new manifestation, and new meaning in his installations. Indeed, the works themselves are all works of persistence and resurrection. Through his astonishingly creative use of materials, his determination to see and use old materials in new ways and to keep dying traditions alive, Robleto resurrects ideas, emotions, and even people, forming and re-forming them into new objects, new ideas, and new emotions. The world of the future will not be the same as the one we live in now, but Robleto invites us to envisage one in which we can take the found objects all around us, the materials we considered obsolete, the things we thought were no longer of any use, and find a way to use them to save ourselves and the other species with whom we share the planet. To fight back against finitude.

Imagine if tomorrow the leaves on the trees failed to rustle. Imagine if the clouds did not drift by. Imagine if a gull never floated on a rising waft of air, or we were never to be relieved by a cool breeze on a sultry day. Were any of these things to happen, we might realize that we had lost the wind. We might feel what this loss meant. And we might wonder how we let such a dreadful thing happen and what, if anything, could be done to get it back.

Climate change will not take away the wind. On the contrary, it may well make it stronger. But it will cause us to lose a great deal of value. To care about this impending loss, to know what it means, we have to *feel* it. Poet Christina Rossetti asked: Who has seen the wind? Dario Robleto has seen the wind. He makes us see it, too. More important, he makes us feel what the world would be like if we no longer had it.

SOURCES

Adams, John Luther. "Global Warming and Art," in *Winter Music: Composing the North*. Wesleyan University Press, 2004.

Berry, Ian, ed. *Dario Robleto: Alloy of Love*. University of Washington Press and The Frances Young Tang Teaching Museum and Art Gallery, Skidmore College: New York, 2008.

Edelstein, Wendy. "Passion and Romance and Love: The Role Artists can Play in Communicating about Climate Change," www.berkeley.edu/news/berkeleyan/2009/05/01_passion.shtml, 2009.

Kope, Beth. *Falling Season*. Leaf Press, 2010.

McLaughlin, John F., Hellmann, Jessica J., Boggs, Carol L. and Ehrlich, Paul R. "Climate Change Hastens Population Extinctions," in Proceedings of the National Academy of Sciences, 99 (9): 6070-6074 www.pnas.org/cgi/doi/10.1073/pnas.052131199, 2002.

Randall, Rosemary. "Loss and Climate Change: The Cost of Parallel Narratives" in *Ecopsychology* 1(3): 118–129. www.bibsonomy.org/bibtex/2d5c93d1647d4cf6fd7d1e2f3389dbaf0/smatthiesen, 2009.

Michelle White

ASSOCIATE CURATOR, THE MENIL COLLECTION, HOUSTON

"When you pull the curtain back, I want to know that something actually happened."[1]

The pain of loss, the romance of a love letter, the poignancy of mourning rituals during wartime, the startling biological capabilities of the human species despite despair or environmental assault, the soulfulness embodied in the lyrics of the blues—these are some of the complex emotions tied to life and death that Dario Robleto has fearlessly tackled throughout his career as an artist. Risky and extraordinary in our cynical age, his exploration is about seeking something of an essential impulse beating in people, ideas, and things. Yet what is even more daring about Robleto's practice is his willingness to base the production of his work on an earnest belief that materials have meaning—that real "stuff" in the world has latent potential that can be activated by the viewer in such a way that it makes an impact

1 Artist in conversation with the author, January 2011.

literally, metaphorically, and even psychologically. Because of this power, the artist's heart-wrenching and heavy themes, related to how and why we feel, often guide conversations about his work. If we take a different approach and first look at how Robleto makes objects, we can see that his scientifically based process, rooted in the rational methods of gathering and questioning knowledge, is paramount. It provides the tangible substance that gives breath to his theoretical ideas and illuminates his investigation of historical temporality, our fragile connections to the past, and art's ability to make a difference.

Robleto's *how* is alchemical. Often labor-intensive, his mysterious processes (which he sometimes hesitates to reveal) involve the transmutation of physical matter in such a way that the chemical conversion does not eliminate the essential building blocks that give the original substance what could be called its soul. For instance, a material the artist frequently takes through this procedure is vinyl records. Molding, melting, and stripping the dark plastic, he reshapes the records into other things: buttons for a shirt, dark marrow injected into a dinosaur bone, flecks of dust pushed into the coarse weave of a blanket. The altered records sometimes bear a faint visual trace of their former lives. In some of his works you can link the mutated black to vinyl's familiar sheen, a slight formal connection that suggests a song's melody or memory is still embedded in the now-mute plastic. Perhaps the lyrical possibilities of music as an emotional agent are not only still there to be comprehended and understood by the audience, but to serve in the same capacity as a ballad might help initiate romance, or an angst-filled rock song might soothe through the commiseration of pain.

Other examples of Robleto's vinyl works contain no visual clues linking the material to its original form because the artist has entirely reshaped the record into something else—something else so convincing in its verisimilitude that the only reference to a record is in the description on the work's label. Yet even with close-to-complete transformation of the material, the artist believes that life—like the emotional pulse of music hidden in the plastic—is still invested in the altered substance, a belief that he asks the viewer to assume in order to conceptually complete the work. The more persuasive the change and the more "real" the object, the bigger the leap we have to take. For this reason, in addition to using the scientific word "transmutation" to describe his method of molecular conversation, the religious word "transubstantiation" is also applicable. Robleto's alchemical change is contingent on the unquantifiable necessity of faith that something real is happening behind the curtain. In other words, his practice is about skating the edge between fact and fiction, science and poetry. He wants magic, but not magic disconnected from quantifiable truth.

As such, Robleto's alchemy is unlike the term's traditional definition in art and literature. For here it is never about actual methods of physical conversion and, by extension, actual goals of resuscitation and healing. Instead, the alchemy tends to serve as many graceful allegories and metaphors. The mythic—if not scientifically preposterous—idea embedded in ancient and clandestine occult practices of turning bubbling pots of melting base metal into gold, for instance, is an ideal way to explain how an artist gives life to a proverbial lump of worthless clay by turning it into a gleaming masterpiece. During the Renaissance, artists were fond of this analogy. In his 16th-century autobiography, artist Benvenuto Cellini describes casting his sculpture of the mythological figure Perseus as a life-imbuing act, a struggle with death and a creative victory of overcoming material restraints.

> "I had someone bring me a lump of pewter, weighing about sixty pounds, which I threw inside the furnace onto the caked metal. By this means, and by piling on the fuel and stirring with pokers and iron bars, the metal soon became molten. ... I had brought a corpse back to life."[2]

In contemporary art, historian James Elkins has argued that the legacy of alchemical symbolism is found in the way artists, and in particular painters, have extended it to obscure meaning. He writes that in the postmodern dance of confusion, "Alchemy is one of the best models for understanding

2 *The Autobiography of Benvenuto Cellini*. Trans. George Bull. London: Penguin Classics, 1956.

the contemporary aversion to full logical or rational sense."[3] That is, artists have used the combination of form and content, word and image, with embedded and hidden meaning to create a case for ambiguity and to deliberately sabotage clear comprehension. In literature, alchemy is also a metaphor. Highly influential to the 20th-century philosophies of Carl Jung, it came to be equated with the existential quest of the individual seeking truth, answers, and higher states of being, epitomized by the character Santiago in Paulo Coelho's popular novel *The Alchemist* (1988). The young protagonist seeks the solution to life's puzzle by traveling afar to learn the magical secret of "the soul of the world." At the end of the journey, he learns that transformation of metal into gold is not literal but inside one's own heart.

Robleto has an entirely different proposition to the ancient allegory. For the artist, alchemy is not a means to talk about something else or a sign of artistic creation, obfuscation, or spiritual symbolism. His alchemy is literal. Rather than alchemical associatives or metaphors, Robleto is interested in the scientific feat of the actual act and the potential of material transformation to be capable of effecting and affirming real change. As curator Nora Burnett

3   Elkins, James. "Four Ways of Measuring the Distance Between Alchemy and Contemporary Art," in *HYLE—International Journal for Philosophy of Chemistry*, Vol. 9, No.1 (2003). pp. 105–118.

4   Burnett Abrams, Nora. *Dario Robleto: An Instinct Toward Life*. Denver: Museum of Contemporary Art Denver, 2011. p. 9.

Abrams has written, Robleto's process "achieve[s] what no fable or fairy tale could do: authenticate real, lived experience."[4] Some of Robleto's earliest examples of this process are works he made by repurposing a nostalgic material from his past so it could serve a redemptive purpose. In *Deeper Into Movies (Buttons, Socks, Teddy Bears & Mittens)* (1997), he unraveled his first baby blanket. After purchasing sewing thread at a fabrics shop, he wound his special thread on the spools and returned the objects to the store. As our imaginations run wild with the potential scenarios involving the unassuming customers, the poignancy is in the artistic process. The labor and care of the action—spooling and unspooling—point to the hope that the comfort the cloth served Robleto could perhaps help someone else in its altered state, a state that literally gives the sentimental material a brand-new life.

Like the thread of a blanket, the curious materials Robleto works with are unlikely, if not incredulous. Always hitched with illustrative adjectives, they read like fairy-tale potions in an apothecary shop and describe the actions the artist has enacted on the substance, letting the viewer peek into his laboratory. In this exhibition alone, the media listed on the labels are a compelling and poetic read: hair lockets made of stretched audiotape, carved bones and bone dust, 19th-century hair flowers, human tears and collected moisture from a melting glacier, velvet, lace, ink, hair from a woolly mammoth, black ink made with crushed particles of glass formed by the ferocious heat of a thunderbolt. Saturated in mysterious origin, the materials play an important role in the artist's work because they explain Robleto's process and locate his work in a material reality.

Yet it is also because of their concrete existence that the material descriptions on the labels paradoxically ask us to suspend belief. Did the thread really come from his dismantled childhood blanky? Is the gray dust truly from the volcanic ash of Mount St. Helens? And where does he find the remains of extinct creatures? Almost rhetorically, the types of questions he forces us to struggle with in light of the assembled objects' exoticism, as well as his feats in gathering and manipulating them, ask us to believe the collected objects are real and that there is dormant life embedded in their fabric. It is a proposition with deep ramifications. If thread, steeped in the warm essence of childhood, can provide some type of hidden power when it is used to mend another garment, can material, and therefore art, serve as an agent of repair?

Robleto's ongoing inquiry and experimentation with the process of material transformation as a catalyst for meaningful change, as well as larger questions about art's efficacy, has led to the ideas he is dealing with in his current work: the fragility of life and the redemptive power of art (in its transformative material magic). As Bellini wrote, art is about giving back life to the corpse and, therefore, time. Indeed, one aspect of ancient alchemy is the pursuit of creating a key to longevity, the well-known fountain of youth. This etymological root plays out in Robleto's recent work about what he calls the boundaries of life—instances where biological odds are defied. For example, his eclectic research has included studies about supercentenarians (people who live to 110 or older), odds-defining survivors of multiple lighting strikes, and the reappearance of extinct species.

Among this group related to survival is *Words Tremble With the Thoughts They Express* (2008). The sculpture consists of an octagonal glass-and-wood vitrine holding delicate feathers that the artist made by stripping and stretching the tape of an audio recording of the last known recitation of now-extinct languages and the sounds of extinct species of birds. For example, the feather the artist has labeled "Lord God Bird" is the colloquial name for the ivory-billed woodpecker. It is a Lazarus species, unlike the other extinct birds included in the work. Rediscovered in the woods of Arkansas in 2005, 60 years after it had been presumed extinct, the bird has never been seen again. Another label reads "Salinan," a Native American dialect spoken in the central-coast region of California until the 1950s. The feathers of lost sounds (which alternate between people and animals) are placed on a bed of volcanic ash from Mount St. Helens (the Washington state volcano that erupted in 1980) and surround a glass inkwell filled with pigment made from ground fulgurites. Explained on the label as "glass produced by lightning strikes when heat from blasts melts surrounding sand," the ink is based on a traditional recipe of grinding soot to make the dark pigment.

Together the ensemble operates like an homage to obsolesce and natural devastation. Yet from the proverbial ash rises life. The feathers are also quills. Surrounding the ink and within a container that resembles a 19th-century portable writing station, they are poised to create new words out of destruction and death. Here again, the artist has created a believable situation where our imagination is stimulated by hypothetical thoughts. What would those sounds—untranslatable and without a written language—express if they could write? As such, the work becomes an elixir. It gives back time to something lost in such a way that the potential application for their revitalization is literal—neither representation nor metaphor. This is Robleto's alchemy.

In Robleto's cut-and-pasted works on paper, he also creates convincing scenarios within the work where redemption is offered to something that is no longer. These include a group of life-size album-cover collages based on his exploration of human survival and coping strategies. *Tales of Theodicies* (2010), emulates the type of poster or advertisement illustrating an album release for a record label, the kind of ephemera that used to be tucked in an album sleeve or posted on the wall of a record store. With the motto "We are all doing time," the religious label produces prison gospel records about themes of salvation from the 1960s, a time of heightened prison reform in the United States when such programs were publically promoted. The title of the work references theodicy, the branch of theology that uses scientific methodologies to essentially prove God's goodness despite the presence of evil in the world. The work's content, however, is entirely fiction. While the artist based the covers on actual historical examples of choir groups, and the form of the work is based on a real album, the text of the song titles, band names, color combinations, and graphics are entirely the creative concept of the artist, assembled by meticulously cutting out all letters, numbers, and motifs from paper and pasting them together.

Adopting DJ vocabulary, Robleto has called this strategy of appropriation remixing and sampling. But his liberal gesture with the past can perhaps more accurately be compared to the literary genre of historical fiction, because Robleto's play with invention is deeply attached to the artist's careful study of historical fact and empathy. In this work on paper, for example, the artist construct was generated in a process that involved positioning himself within the referenced time and location in order to ask himself questions like, "What would I sing in a predicament of entrapment?" and "What is the meaning of salvation during a condition of deep regret or inner battles with the nature of evil?"

Alchemical Gardens (2009), is another work on paper. Like the artist's series of imaginary records, it is a collaged fabrication involving a pastiche of actual historical traditions that related to the endurance of the human species. Here, the topic is defiant gardens, also known as war gardens or victory gardens. A type of mourning ritual or coping mechanism, the gardens are grown in extraordinary and difficult circumstances and common during wartime: on battlefields, on mass graves, or in destitute communities. Symbolic and life-affirming, the gardens declare that hope can come out of despair and violence, and often serve as signs of protest. Some historical examples include gardens grown in Polish ghettos during Nazi occupation, in U.S. internment camps for Japanese-Americans during World War II, and more recently in Iraq.[5] In 2009, the *New York Times* reported on a defiant gardener in Baghdad. Through his topiary sculpture of eagles, he brought color and beauty to a desolate city destroyed by conflict.[6]

In this tableau, instead of record covers, Robleto has constructed a sponsorship board for a community garden center called "Alchemical Gardens." Like advertisements for county ecology clubs and civic groups offering gardening workshops, the work is peppered with textual references

5 For more examples, see Kenneth I. Helphand, *Defiant Gardens: Making Gardens in Wartime.* San Antonio: Trinity University Press, 2006.

6 Leland, John. "Fanciful Gardens Emerge in a City of Tan and Gray," *New York Times*, November 1, 2009.

to the subversive practice of sustaining life by growing. As such, the artistic translation of this (remixed) history emphasizes the transformative, if not alchemical, power of the garden for suffering peoples. Much like the silence of Robleto's sculpture with mute vinyl and lost audiotape of extinct noise, the effect of these works on paper becomes the evocation of sounds and stories that can only be sung or told if constructed in the head of the viewer. It is a conceptual conversion that makes Robleto's work with paper, in comparison to his sculptural work, especially compelling because it verges more closely with traditional or flat methods of representation. Unlike his sculptures, the paper works are not made with the types of actual objects that are magically imbued with former meaning and life, like bones, dust, and liquids collected from far-flung locations. Instead, material transformation with paper and scissors skirts the boundaries of possibility, for here the artist's real desire to give back life through his work is happening in the resurrection of an idea.

Robleto's sincerity in grappling with questions about art's potential via push and pull with fact and fiction is relevant. What could be more anachronistic, yet more revealing of our own skepticism, than the faith of an artist who believes in something real now, and works of art that address our own difficulties in surmounting this obstacle of doubt while creating tangible change? His intentional reluctance to fully shine light on how he bends, prods, and transforms actual materials, and his careful gestures that prevent his work from entering an entirely imaginary if not religious realm, create an atmosphere of ambiguity, a space that beautifully allows for what the artist hopes is real magic. In the literal and visual tropes that have discussed, adopted, or addressed the alchemical processes, physical failure is inevitable. Johannes Trithemius, a 16th-century philosopher and skeptic of the art of alchemy, famously compared it to "a chaste prostitute who has many lovers but disappoints all and grants her favors to none. She transforms haughty into fools, the rich into paupers, the philosophers into dolts, and the deceived into loquacious deceivers."[7] Robleto is proposing an alternative. By pulling back the curtain and showing us that something actually can happen when he makes, he is paradoxically fulfilling the most cherished and elusive aspiration of both art and alchemy: belief.

7   Johannes Trithemius, as quoted by Umberto Eco, *Foucault's Pendulum*. University of Michigan, 1989. p. 331.

EXHIBITION CHECKLIST

THE ARK OF FRAILTY 2008

Poplar, typeset on cardstock, hair lockets made
of stretched and curled audiotape recordings of
"Lazarus species" (species that are rediscovered
alive after being classified extinct) in the wild,
19th-century hair flowers, 19th-century dried
flowers, lace and fabric from widows' mourning
dresses, colored paper, silk, antique ribbon and
buttons, carved animal bone buttons, homemade
paper, willow, ash, white oak, milk paint, glass
71 ½ x 15 ¾ x 105 ¼ inches
Courtesy of the artist and Inman Gallery,
Houston, Texas

THE BOUNDARY OF LIFE IS QUIETLY CROSSED 2008

Ink-dyed poplar, typeset on cardstock, hair lockets
made of stretched and curled audiotape recordings
of supercentenarians (humans living to 110 or
older), 19th-century hair flowers, lace and fabric
from widows' mourning dresses, colored paper,
silk, antique ribbon, homemade paper, willow,
ash, white oak, milk paint, glass
71 ½ x 15 ½ x 104 ½ inches
Courtesy of the artist and Inman Gallery,
Houston, Texas

THE COMMON DENOMINATOR OF EXISTENCE
IS LOSS 2008

50,000-year-old extinct cave bear paws, human
hand bones, stretched and pulled audiotape of
the earliest audio recording of time (experimental
clock, 1878), 19th-century mourning ribbon, bocote,
shellac, glass
42 ¾ x 47 ½ x 47 ½ inches
Collection of Nancy and Stanley Singer, East
Hampton, New York

A HOMEOPATHIC TREATMENT FOR
HUMAN LONGING 2008

Glass vials, vintage glass electrode wands,
19th-century bloodletting cupping glass, various
artist-made homeopathic remedies (sound of glaciers
melting, voice of oldest to ever live, last heartbeats of
loved one, million-year-old blossom, million-year-old
raindrop, deceased lovers' heartbeats, extinct animal
sounds, extinct languages), various custom-ordered
remedies made by professional homeopath (black amber,
willow, tears, mammoth hair, glacial runoff, voice of
oldest widow, black swan bone dust, Sylvia Plath's voice),
velvet, silk, leather, ribbon, brass, iron, cork, pine, typeset
66 x 129 x 53 ¼ inches
Courtesy of the artist and D'Amelio Terras,
New York, New York

SOME LONGINGS SURVIVE DEATH 2008

Glacially released 50,000-year-old woolly mammoth
tusks, 19th-century braided hair flowers of various
lovers intertwined with glacially released woolly
mammoth hair, carved ivory and bone, bocote, colored
paper, silk, ribbon, typeset
57 x 8 x 53 inches
Courtesy of the artist and ACME. Gallery,
Los Angeles, California

WORDS TREMBLE WITH THE THOUGHTS
THEY EXPRESS 2008

Feathers made from stretched audiotape of the last
recordings of now-extinct birds and now-extinct
languages, glass inkwell, homemade ink (lamp black,
ground fulgurites [glass produced by lightning strikes
when heat from the blast melts surrounding sand],
cuttlefish sepia), homemade paper, volcanic ash from
Mount St. Helens, ink-dyed willow, brass, typeset
63 ¾ x 25 ½ x 24 ½ inches
Courtesy of the artist and Inman Gallery,
Houston, Texas

ALCHEMICAL GARDENS 2009

Cut paper, colored pencil, foam core, glue

52 ¼ x 36 ¾ x 3 ½inches

Courtesy of the artist and ACME. Gallery,

Los Angeles, California

FOLKS ON THE FRINGE 2009

Cut paper, colored pencil, foam core, glue

52 ¼ x 36 ¾ x 3 ½ inches

Collection of Bridget and Patrick Wade,

Houston, Texas

SOCIETY OF SEEKERS 2009

Cut paper, colored pencil, foam core, glue

52 ¼ x 36 ¾ x 3 ½inches

Courtesy of the artist and ACME. Gallery,

Los Angeles, California

MAIDENS OF MOTHER'S MILK THISTLE 2009

Cut paper, colored pencil, foam core, glue

52 ¼ x 36 ¾ x 3 ½ inches

Courtesy of the artist and ACME. Gallery,

Los Angeles, California

DEFIANT GARDENS 2009–2010

Cut paper, homemade paper (pulp made from

soldiers' letters sent home and wife/sweetheart letters

sent to soldiers from various wars, cotton), carrier

pigeon skeletons, World War II-era pigeon message

capsules, dried flowers from various battlefields,

hair flowers braided by war widows, mourning dress

fabric, excavated shrapnel and bullet lead from

various battlefields, various seeds, various seashells,

cartes de visites, gold leaf, silk, ribbon, wood, glass,

foam core, glue

79 ½ x 61 x 4 ½ inches

Courtesy of the artist; ACME. Gallery, Los Angeles,

California; Inman Gallery, Houston, Texas; and

D'amelio Terras, New York, New York

TALES OF THEODICIES 2010

Cut paper, cut album cover elements, colored

pencil, ribbon, foam core, glue

85 x 70 x 1 inches

Courtesy of the artist and ACME. Gallery,

Los Angeles, California

CANDLES UN-BURN, SUNS UN-SHINE,
DEATH UN-DIES 2011

Inkjet print on custom vinyl wall paper,

61° curved wall

A collection of stage lights taken from the

album covers of live performances of

now-deceased musicians

10 x 22 ½ feet

Courtesy of the artist and D'Amelio Terras,

New York, New York

ACKNOWLEDGMENTS

Gilbert Vicario

I would like to thank Dario Robleto for allowing me into his world. I have gotten to know him and his work over the course of the past seven years, eagerly following his train of thought and quickly becoming part of his ever-expanding community. The exhibition at the Des Moines Art Center is the realization of many years devoted to thinking about his practice and seeing how that could be articulated in a thoughtful yet concentrated manner. There is a profound density of ideas and aesthetics that comprise his work, and it has been a challenge to highlight and clarify those that clearly define him as a crucial contemporary voice. *Survival Does Not Lie In The Heavens* demonstrates Robleto's abiding interest in getting to the core of who we are as humans—our thoughts, our ambitions, our vulnerabilities—and how that leaves a physical imprint on the world around us. This is the right moment to present his work, and I am grateful for the Des Moines Art Center's willingness to support challenging and complex artistic visions such as his.

At the Art Center I would first like to thank Jeff Fleming, director, a keen supporter of Robleto's work for many years. The Art Center staff including Mickey Koch, associate registrar; Jay Ewart, chief preparator; and his staff, Jill Featherstone, museum education director; Christine Doolittle, marketing and public relations director; and Emily Bahnsen, development director. I would like to thank Nancy and Stanley Singer of East Hampton, New York, and Bridget and Patrick Wade of Houston, Texas, for their willingness to lend key works to the exhibition. I would like to give special thanks to Kerry Inman of Inman Gallery in Houston for her generosity, support, and enthusiasm for this exhibition, along with Patrick Reynolds, also at Inman Gallery. I would like to acknowledge another early supporter, Lucien Terras of D'Amelio Terras in New York City, for his support and enthusiasm for this exhibition as well as Randy Sommer of ACME. Gallery in Los Angeles for his assistance and support. Thank you to Image Transform and Justin Boyd for their technical assistance on the *Candles Un-burn* installation. I am appreciative to Naomi Oreskes, professor of history at the University of California, San Diego, and Michelle White, associate curator at The Menil Collection in Houston, for their important contributions to the exhibition publication. And appreciative to those who worked on the catalogue: Carrie Schmitz, copy editor; Connie McAllister for her keen eye; and, last but not least, a warm thank you to Connie Wilson, graphic designer for conceiving a fitting editorial counterpart to the exhibition.

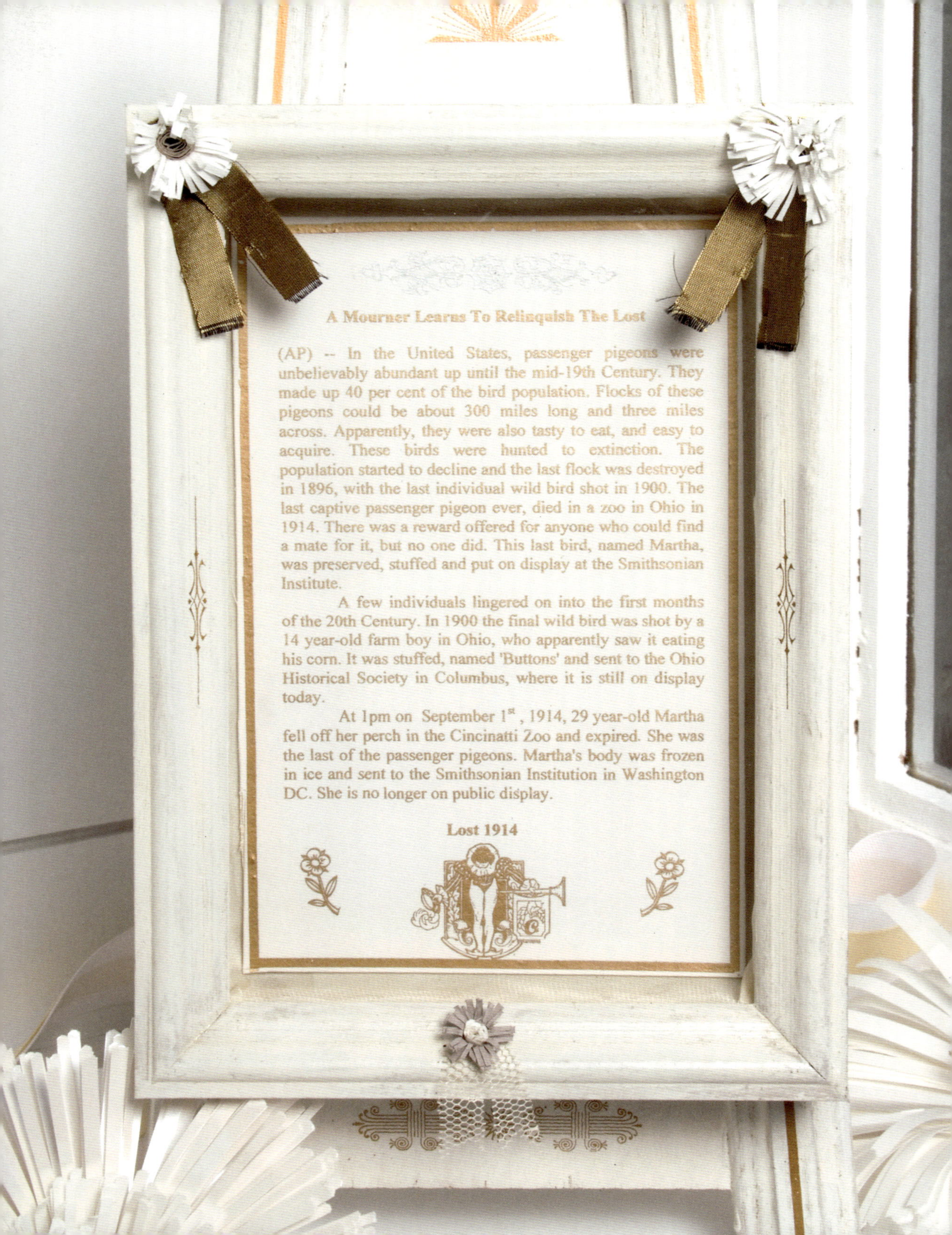

A Mourner Learns To Relinquish The Lost

(AP) -- In the United States, passenger pigeons were unbelievably abundant up until the mid-19th Century. They made up 40 per cent of the bird population. Flocks of these pigeons could be about 300 miles long and three miles across. Apparently, they were also tasty to eat, and easy to acquire. These birds were hunted to extinction. The population started to decline and the last flock was destroyed in 1896, with the last individual wild bird shot in 1900. The last captive passenger pigeon ever, died in a zoo in Ohio in 1914. There was a reward offered for anyone who could find a mate for it, but no one did. This last bird, named Martha, was preserved, stuffed and put on display at the Smithsonian Institute.

A few individuals lingered on into the first months of the 20th Century. In 1900 the final wild bird was shot by a 14 year-old farm boy in Ohio, who apparently saw it eating his corn. It was stuffed, named 'Buttons' and sent to the Ohio Historical Society in Columbus, where it is still on display today.

At 1pm on September 1st, 1914, 29 year-old Martha fell off her perch in the Cincinatti Zoo and expired. She was the last of the passenger pigeons. Martha's body was frozen in ice and sent to the Smithsonian Institution in Washington DC. She is no longer on public display.

Lost 1914

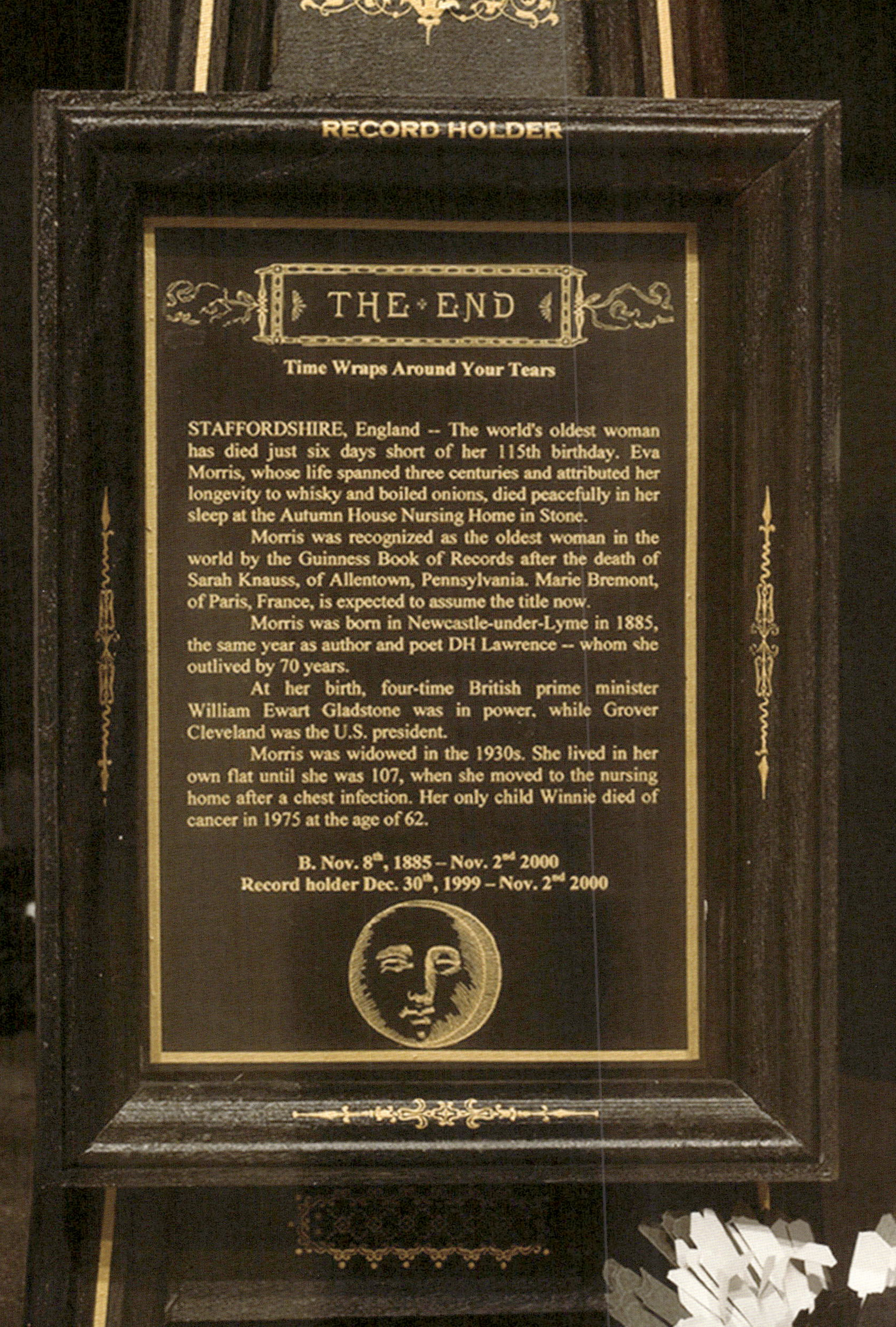

RECORD HOLDER

THE · END

Time Wraps Around Your Tears

STAFFORDSHIRE, England -- The world's oldest woman has died just six days short of her 115th birthday. Eva Morris, whose life spanned three centuries and attributed her longevity to whisky and boiled onions, died peacefully in her sleep at the Autumn House Nursing Home in Stone.

Morris was recognized as the oldest woman in the world by the Guinness Book of Records after the death of Sarah Knauss, of Allentown, Pennsylvania. Marie Bremont, of Paris, France, is expected to assume the title now.

Morris was born in Newcastle-under-Lyme in 1885, the same year as author and poet DH Lawrence -- whom she outlived by 70 years.

At her birth, four-time British prime minister William Ewart Gladstone was in power, while Grover Cleveland was the U.S. president.

Morris was widowed in the 1930s. She lived in her own flat until she was 107, when she moved to the nursing home after a chest infection. Her only child Winnie died of cancer in 1975 at the age of 62.

B. Nov. 8th, 1885 – Nov. 2nd 2000
Record holder Dec. 30th, 1999 – Nov. 2nd 2000

DARIO ROBLETO: SURVIVAL DOES NOT LIE IN THE HEAVENS

ORGANIZED BY Gilbert Vicario

September 23, 2011 – January 15, 2012 / Anna K. Meredith Gallery

ISBN: 9781879003613
Library of Congress Control Number: 20011934838

© Des Moines Art Center
All rights reserved.

No part of this publication may be reproduced or distributed in
any form without the prior written permission of the publisher.

Des Moines Art Center
4700 Grand Avenue / Des Moines, Iowa 50312
515.277.4405 / desmoinesartcenter.org

DESIGN: Connie Wilson Design
COPY EDITING: Carrie Schmitz
PRINTING: Shapco Printing, Inc., Minneapolis, Minnesota

This project is supported in part by an award from the National Endowment for the Arts and Wells Fargo.

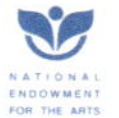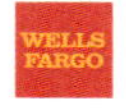

All images © the artist
PHOTO CREDITS Pages 7, 57, 71: Eric Hester / Pages 10, 12, 14, 19: Ansen Seale
Pages 33, 53: Robert Wedemeyer / Pages 38–39, 46–47, 68, 75: Sibila Savage / Pages 44–45: Thomas R. DuBrock
Pages 58–59, 76: Pablo Mason / All other images by the artist.

PAGE 118–119
Details from **THE BOUNDARY OF LIFE IS QUIETLY CROSSED** and **THE ARK OF FRAILTY**

EXCERPTS FROM THE SERIES
THE SKY, ONCE CHOKED WITH STARS, WILL SLOWLY DARKEN 2011

OPPOSITE TITLE PAGE Johnny Cash / *Johnny Cash At San Quentin*
OPPOSITE TABLE OF CONTENTS Jimi Hendrix / *In Concert*
PAGE 4 Sun Ra / *Live At The Ann Arbor Blues & Jazz Festival*
PAGE 82 Rick Nelson / *In Concert*
PAGE 100 John Coltrane / Archie Shepp / *New Thing At Newport*